The Liver Rescue Cookbook

Liver Rescue Diet with Life-changing Foods for Everyone to Lose Weight Permanently, Cure Fatty Liver, Have Better Skin and Live Better

By Carol Lewis

Warning-Disclaimer

The purpose of this book is to educate and entertain. The author or publisher does not guarantee that anyone following the techniques, suggestions, tips, ideas, or strategies will become successful. The author and publisher shall have neither liability or responsibility to anyone with respect to any loss or damage caused, or alleged to be caused, directly or indirectly by the information contained in this book.

Contents

Introduction

Fatty liver and other liver problems are serious issues that can lead to liver damage, cirrhosis, and liver failure which if left untreated will result in irreversible damage and life-threatening conditions. This is why it's important to take charge of your health and stop putting things off once and for all. Luckily for you, there is an answer that can solve your problems and it's in this book.

Would you like to eat scrumptious meals and cleanse your liver problems simultaneously? A healthy liver is essential for a healthy life! And your main weapon to clean your liver is the food you put inside your body. Having a diet geared for you is one of the most effective ways to cure fatty liver and other liver problems. And in this book, you will discover the natural cure to fatty liver and proven procedures to help reverse and prevent liver problems permanently.

In this book, you will find specially chosen recipes formulated to help people suffering from liver disease. Following this uniquely tailored diet will certainly improve your liver conditions.

Once again, I thank you for purchasing this book and hope that after this book your liver will undergo miracles. Now is the time to properly treat your liver. Don't wait another minute. If you're ready to start cleansing your liver, turn to the next page!

Chapter 1: Essentials About the Liver

The liver is one of the most important human organs and performs up to 500 different functions for your body. In this chapter, you will learn all the essentials of the liver and what it does to the body which includes:

- What is the Liver and What Does it Do?
- The Connection Between Liver Health, Weight Loss and Stubborn Fat
- A List of Liver Problems
- What are the Early Signs and Causes of Liver Problems?

Let's get started.

What is the Liver and What Does It Do?

Your liver is the star player of the body and many people don't quite understand just how important this organ is. The liver is located in the right upper abdomen below the diaphragm and weighs 3 pounds. Your liver is the most metabolically active and most complex organ that you possess. It performs over 500 different functions, in fact, most of them are currently unknown to modern science. Some of the major ones include:

- Your liver plays an essential role in the metabolism of carbs, fats, and protein.
- The liver helps process alcohol and flush toxins from our bodies.
- The liver processes fat and protects the pancreas
- It is responsible for storing glucose, glycogen, vitamins, and minerals.
- It disarms and detains harmful substances.
- It screens and filters the blood from most drugs, alcohol, and chemicals and provide you with its own immune function.
- Converts and store extra glucose in the form of glycogen, which provides energy during times of starvation.
- It helps protect you from infection which is the reason why infections are more likely to occur if the liver is damaged.

- Your liver excretes bile into the intestine. Bile is essential for absorbing fats and removing toxic waste.

As you already know, this book is meant to help readers fight and prevent liver disease through diet and lifestyle changes. Anything that prevents your liver from performing normal can be identified as liver disease. There are many different types of liver disease, but liver damage all takes the same route. Whether your liver is contaminated with a virus, injured by chemical substances, or under attack from your own immune system, the underlying danger is the same – that if your liver becomes damaged to such a degree it can no longer function to keep you alive. Here we will cover the stages of liver disease:

IN A HEALTHY LIVER: Your liver will function normally and help keep infections at bay. It also helps clean your body, monitors your blood and absorbs food which is then used for energy later. A healthy liver has the remarkable ability to regenerate upon damage. Anything that hinders your liver from functioning properly or prevents it from regenerating after injury is a cause of serious concern.

UPON INFLAMMATION: Inflammation in the liver is the early stage of any liver disease. Inflammation causes the liver to turn enlarged, stressed and tender. Inflammation means that your body is trying to fight off an infection or heal from an injury. But consistent inflammation can result in permanent liver damage. You can often feel when some parts of your become inflamed. However, in some cases, an inflamed liver may not give any hints of discomfort. If a health professional diagnosed your liver disease and treat it successfully, it will go away with no problems.

AFTER INFLAMMATION: If inflammation goes untreated, your liver will begin a scaring process known as fibrosis. Fibrosis is when healthy liver tissue is replaced with scar tissue. If fibrosis occurs, your liver cannot keep up with its many duties. As more scar tissue continues to build up, your liver may not be at its optimal performance. If a health professional can diagnose and successfully treat you during this stage, your liver may return back to normal over time.

CIRRHOSIS: When hard scar tissue replaces soft healthy scar tissue this is known as cirrhosis. As it continues to worsen, healthy tissue begins to deplete. If cirrhosis is ignored and not treated by a health professional, it will result in liver failure and will not be able to function at all. Cirrhosis can also cause a host of complications such as liver cancer. Some signs to be on the lookout for include:

- Easy to bleed or bruise
- A build-up of water in your legs or abdomen.
- Yellow color skin and eyes
- Itching

If you have been diagnosed with cirrhosis, treatment will be concentrated on preventing the condition from getting severe. It may be impossible to cure or slow down the liver damage. But you can still stop the healthy liver tissue from scarring.
LIVER FAILURE: When your liver loses all its function, this life-threatening condition is known as liver failure and it requires urgent medical care. The first symptoms of liver failure include:

- Loss of appetite
- Abdomen pain
- Fatigue
- Diarrhea
- Nausea

Due to the fact that these symptoms can mean different things, it can be hard to determine if your liver is actually failing. But if liver failure progresses, the symptoms become more prominent. Those at risk may feel disoriented and extremely tired. Treatment is required during liver failure. Health professionals will try to scavenge the parts of your liver still functioning. If this doesn't work, the alternative option will be a liver transplant.
I highly recommend scheduling an appointment with your primary doctor to check the current condition of your liver.

All Kinds of Liver Problems

There are more than 100 identifiable types of liver disease, all of whom are caused by different sets of factors, including infections, toxic compounds, genetics, alcohol consumption, and other unknown causes. Here we will learn about the many problems that can develop in your liver and things to discuss with your doctor.
ALAGILLE SYNDROME: Alagille syndrome is a genetical disorder that causes liver damage due to an abnormal composition of the bile ducts.
ALCOHOL-RELATED LIVER DISEASE:A liver disease caused by drinking too much alcohol is pretty common. Moderate drinking can drastically reduce your risk of the disease. Excessive consumptions of alcohol will seriously affect your health. Not only will it damage your liver but it can affect your mood, behavior, and disrupt your ability to think rationally. The three main culprits of this disease include:

- **FATTY LIVER:** A fat build up inside your liver cells which makes hinders your liver from functioning normally.
- **ALCOHOLIC HEPATITIS:** Your liver becomes inflamed or swelled.
- **CIRRHOSIS:** Cirrhosis is when hard nonliving tissue begins to replace healthy liver tissue.

ALPHA-1 ANTITRYPSIN: Alpha-1 antitrypsin also known as AAT deficiency s a hereditary disorder that may lead to liver disease.

AUTOIMMUNE HEPATITIS: Autoimmune hepatitis is a disease where your immune system starts to attack your own liver in which it can result in liver inflammation and liver damage. Health professionals do not know what causes this disease.

BENIGN LIVER TUMORS: A common liver problem where a noncancerous tumor forms in the liver. Benign liver tumors are not fatal but may cause discomfort.

BILIARY ATRESIA: Biliary atresia is a rare condition that only occurs in infants. It is when the bile ducts of the liver are scarred and blocked.

GILBERT'S SYNDROME: Gilbert's syndrome is a common liver condition who doesn't pose any health risks. It is a condition in which your liver doesn't process bilirubin substance properly. It typically doesn't require medical treatment.

HEMOCHROMATOSIS: Hemochromatosis occurs when you eat foods with too much iron. When you eat too much iron, it is stored in your liver, pancreas, and heart. Excessive iron can cause serious damage in your liver. Without medical treatment, hemochromatosis can result in liver failure.

HEPATITIS: Hepatitis is when your liver becomes inflamed. There are different classifications for hepatitis:

- **HEPATITIS A:** Hepatitis A can occur if you come into contact with the hepatitis A virus via eating food or drinking water polluted by their feces.
- **HEPATITIS B:** Hepatitis B can occur if you come into contact with the body fluids of the person who has hepatitis B virus via blood, semen, urine or vaginal secretions. Unprotected sex and sharing personal hygiene products can increase your risk of acquiring hepatitis B.
- **HEPATITIS C:** Hepatitis C occurs if you come into direct contact with those with this disease via drug injection or sexual contact.
- **HEPATITIS D:** Hepatitis D is more severe to your liver and can be transmitted by direct contact with blood.

LIVER CANER: The growth and spread of infectious cells in your liver are known as liver cancer. Cancer that ignites in your liver is known as primary liver cancer. Cancer that spreads to the liver from a different organ is known as metastatic liver cancer. Untreated cirrhosis, Hepatitis B and C most often lead to liver cancer along with excessive alcohol use.

NON-ALCOHOLIC FATTY LIVER DISEASE: This disease is similar to fatty liver disease where a fat accumulation occurs in your liver however this one is not induced by alcohol.

The Early Signs and Causes of Liver Problems

Although the liver is located inside the body, there are some signs and symptoms that may suggest problems are arising:

- Lack of appetite
- Binge eating
- Very dark or brown-colored urine
- Strong urine smell
- Abdominal swelling
- Nausea and vomiting
- Always feeling tired, weak and fatigued
- Yellowing of the skin and eyes
- Itchy skin
- Spider angiomas
- Easy bruising
- Bad breath
- Blemishes, acne, and hyperpigmentation appearing on your face and other parts of your body
- Red palms
- Brain fog and difficulty trying to focus

What causes liver problems?

A host of factors can contribute to the development of liver disease which includes:

- Exposure to bacteria, viruses, and infections
- Immune system abnormality
- Genetics
- Cancer
- Fat accumulation in the liver
- Heavy alcohol use

- Needle sharing
- Tattoos and piercing have been associated with liver damage and hepatitis due to non-sterile equipment
- Unprotected unsafe sex
- Blood transfusions, blood products or organ donations before June 1992
- Contact with another person’s blood, saliva, and other bodily fluids
- Unclean environment
- Diabetes
- Excessive weight gain and obesity
- Exposure to toxic chemicals and substances

Chapter 2: The Liver Rescue Diet

The most effective treatment for liver problems and fatty liver includes making changes in your diet and exercise, however, some people may need to consult a doctor for other treatments. In this chapter, you will learn everything there is to know about the liver rescue diet which includes:

- What is the Liver Rescue Diet and How Does it Work?
- How to Detoxify the Liver for Weight Loss?
- Other Ways to Keep Your Liver Healthy

If you're ready, let's go on!

What is the Liver Rescue Diet and How Does It Work?

Currently, there are minimal medical treatments that can fight off nonalcoholic fatty liver disease. Thus, following a nutrient-dense diet and an exercise regimen is the best way to counteract liver disease. The liver rescue diet is an effective treatment for liver disease, whether it's alcohol-induced or not, it is geared toward improving liver function through the foods you eat.

A healthy liver helps take out toxins from your body and produce the digestive protein bile. Liver disease will work its way to destroy the liver and prevent it from functioning normally. Liver patients need to have their diet specially adjusted to meet their individual requirements. Talk to a health professional about the best route to take for helping the liver. For most people, the liver rescue diet consists of:

- Tons of fruits and vegetables packed with plant compounds and antioxidants that are optimal towards protecting your liver from dangerous toxins.
- Plants that are loaded with fiber such as legumes and whole grains.
- Meals that contain minimal to zero sugar, salt, trans fats, saturated fats, and refined carbs.

So, what should you avoid on the liver rescue diet? You will avoid foods that negatively impact your liver. Foods that overwork your liver and foods high in toxins all need to be cut off. You will restrict foods that have high contents in fat, sugar, and salt. Also, fried foods and fast foods from restaurants are restricted. Raw or undercooked oysters and clams are a definitive no due to bacteria. Obviously, alcohol needs to be avoided at all cost.

DOES THE LIVER RESCUE DIET ACTUALLY WORK?

Yes, the liver rescue diet has been proven to help people suffering from liver disease improve their liver function and help restore their lives back to normal. All it takes is commitment and following the very specific dietary guidelines. But so that you know, there is no single food that can magically turn your liver to a healthy one. For most individuals, avoiding very fatty foods and alcohol is opportune in avoiding liver damage.

Another thing you should know is that the liver rescue diet cannot replace proper medical treatment. It is always recommended to talk with your primary care doctor about what routes to take in healing your liver otherwise serious underlying medical issues can appear.

How to Detoxify the Liver for Weight Loss?

Your liver helps detoxify compounds that enter your system. This means it has to remove toxins that enter your body from the environment. It has to process and detoxify any medications. It has to remove toxins from the foods and drinks you consume. And it has to take out toxins from bad lifestyle habits such as smoking, drinking, caffeinated beverages, and alcohol.

Here we will learn how to detoxify your liver so it can enhance its effectiveness of this job. During the liver detox, you will be following strict dietary guidelines that promote liver detoxification.

STARTING YOUR DAY

At the beginning of each day, drink a large glass of filtered water. Then, wait 1 hour before drinking this liver cleansing beverage. To make the beverage add the following to a blender:

- 1 cup of citrus juice
- 1 medium garlic clove, peeled
- 1 tablespoon of extra-virgin olive oil
- inch piece of ginger, peeled
- 8-ounces of filtered water

Drink the beverage above and follow it with 1 glass of organic citrus juice. Each ingredient contains antioxidants and liver boosting compounds that can help flush out harmful substances lurking in your liver.

LIVER FLUSH TEA

There are a wide variety of teas that can help detox your liver. Consider adding the following ingredients through your juicer and drink the resulting beverage:

- Milk thistle
- Dandelion root
- Burdock
- Artichokes
- Cardamom seed
- Cinnamon bark
- Juniper berries
- Licorice root
- Fennel seed
- Ginger root
- Clove buds
- Uva ursi
- Black peppercorns
- Orange peel
- Fenugreek seed
- Sassafras root bark
- Parsley root

The procedure to make the liver flush tea is simple, just follow these simple instructions:

- Choose your ingredients and chop them up coarsely.
- Add the chopped ingredients to a juicer
- Heat 1 cup of water on the stove and mix gently with the juice mixture.
- Drink up!

THE LIVER DETOX DIET

For five days, you need to follow a healthy diet geared for one purpose – to detoxify your liver. In order to get started, look at an example of a liver detox diet below:

DAY ONE AND DAY FIVE

After drinking your daily detox tea, you must opt-in for raw, fresh fruits and vegetables. You can drink homemade fruit or vegetable juices as well with no added sweetener. If you choose to eat salads, don't add any store-bought high-sugary dressings instead go for something simple such as olive oil or lemon. Don't eat too much for dinner, a fresh berry smoothie and soy milk will suffice.

DAY TWO, DAY THREE, AND DAY FOUR

During these days you must consume any solid foods. Drink plenty of diluted fruit juice, herbal tea or potassium broth throughout the day.

Chapter 3: Advices of Food for Liver Rescue Diet

One of the best ways to treat any liver disease is with diet. Thus, knowing what you should be eating and what you should not be eating is vitally important to maintain a healthy liver. Overall, the liver rescue diet consists of the following food groups:

- Eat plenty of anti-inflammatory foods such as dark leafy greens
- Eat plenty of fruits high in antioxidants
- Plants packed with fiber such as legumes and whole grains
- Fish and seafood
- Herbal tea
- Low to no consumption of alcohol, added sugar, fried foods, refined carbs, saturated fats, trans fats, and red meat.

This diet can not only help you reverse liver disease but can help you manage weight and prevent the future development of such severe conditions. In Chapter 3, we will learn which foods to incorporate into your diet for liver health and which foods to avoid.

Foods Good for Liver Health

The list below consists of the best foods that promotes liver health and can help cleanse the liver. There is no better way to keep your liver healthy and functioning well but through eating the chosen foods. I highly recommend you fill your plate with one of these liver cleansing foods and to help you do that, you will find some tasty recipes that features such ingredients later on.

BEST HEALING VEGETABLES AND FRUIT FOR LIVER HEALTH

- Apples
- Apricots
- Artichokes
- Arugula
- Asparagus
- Atlantic sea vegetables
- Avocadoes
- Beetroot – Beetroot is abundant in

nitrates and antioxidants are known as betalains, which promotes heart health and decrease inflammation along with oxidative damage.

- Berries (blueberries, raspberries, cranberries, blackberries, etc.) – Berries have always been linked to numerous health benefits due to its high antioxidant content.
- Broccoli -
- Brussel sprouts
- Carrots
- Celery
- Cherries
- Cilantro
- Coconut
- Cruciferous vegetables – Cruciferous vegetables such as broccoli, mustard greens, and brussel sprouts are packed with fiber and advantageous compounds which can shield your liver from damage and increase your levels of detoxification enzymes.
- Cucumbers
- Dandelion greens
- Dates
- Eggplant
- Figs
- Garlic – Garlic is an ultimate detoxifying vegetable that can help keep your liver healthy. Garlic is abundant in an antioxidant called allicin which can help shield your body from oxidative damage.
- Grapefruit – Grapefruit contains many antioxidants such as naringin and naringenin which can naturally shield your liver.
- Grapes – Studies performed on animals and several humans have found that the consumption of grapes and grape seed extract can fight inflammation, raise antioxidant levels and defend the liver from any harm
- Hot peppers
- Sunchokes
- Kale
- Kiwis
- Leafy greens
- Lemons and limes
- Mangoes
- Melons
- Mushrooms
- Onions and scallions
- Oranges and tangerines
- Papayas
- Parsley
- Peaches and nectarines
- Prickly pears – Prickly pears and pear juice can shield your liver from damage induced by consuming alcohol.
- Pineapple
- Dragon fruit
- Pomegranates
- Potatoes
- Radishes
- Pure raw honey

- Red cabbage
- Seaweed
- Spinach
- Sprouts and microgreens
- Sweet potatoes
- Tomatoes
- Fresh turmeric
- Wild blueberries
- Winter squash
- Zucchini

BEST FATTY FISH

Fatty fish is an excellent source for omega-3 fatty acids which are healthy fats that decrease inflammation and have been linked with a lower chance of developing heart disease. You can find fatty fish from the following:

- Wild-caught salmon
- Arctic char
- Mackerel
- Sardines
- Sablefish/Black Cod
- Anchovies
- Rainbow trout
- Albacore tuna
- Pacific halibut
- Rockfish
- Catfish

LEAN PROTEIN

Your body requires some form of protein to stay healthy. You can get your protein from small quantities from meats and poultry. You can also get your protein from legumes, nuts, seeds, tofu, and soy milk if you are a vegetarian.

BEST HEALING HERBS AND SUPPLEMENTS FOR LIVER HEALTH

- 5-MTHF (5-methyltetrahydrofolate)
- ALA (alpha lipoic acid)
- Aloe Vera
- Amla berry
- Ashwagandha
- Barley grass juice powder
- B-complex
- Black walnut
- Burdock root
- Cardamom
- Cat's claw
- Chaga mushroom
- Chicory root
- Coenzyme Q10
- Curcumin
- Dandelion root
- D-mannose
- EPA and DHA
- Eyebright
- Ginger
- Ginseng
- Glutathione
- Goldenseal
- Hibiscus
- Lemon balm
- Licorice root

- L-lysine
- Magnesium glycinate
- Melatonin
- Milk thistle
- MSM
- Mullein leaf
- NAC (N-acetyl cysteine)
- Nascent iodine
- Nettle leaf
- Olive leaf
- Oregon grape root
- Peppermint
- Raspberry leaf
- Red clover
- Rose hips
- Schisandra berry
- Selenium
- Spirulina
- Turmeric
- Vitamin B12
- Vitamin C
- Vitamin D3 Wild blueberry powder
- Yellow dock
- Zinc

BEST BEVERAGES FOR LIVER HEALTH

- Water – Of course, water is good for everything! It helps prevents your body from getting dehydrated and allows your liver to work better.
- Black coffee – Research has found that drinking coffee can help alleviate liver damage and reduces the risk of cirrhosis. In addition, coffee can help decrease inflammation while increasing your antioxidant levels in your liver.
- Blood orange juice – Blood orange juice can help prevent fatty liver disease.
- Tea – It has been widely known that drinking tea is good for your health, but research has shown that it has profound impacts on the liver. In particular, green and black tea improve liver enzyme levels and also reduces oxidative stress.
- Noni fruit juice – Drinking noni fruit juice can help shield your liver from any harm caused by harmful toxins.

OTHER FOODS GOOD FOR LIVER HEALTH

- Olive oil – Olive oil is a healthy fat due to its multitude of health benefits, especially its profound impacts on your metabolic health and heart. Research has also found increase consumptions of olive oil can lower fat in your liver, improves enzymes levels in the liver and amplify blood flow.
- Nuts – Nuts have high-fat contents and are nutritious. Increased nut consumption has been linked to better liver enzymes levels for people suffering from non-alcoholic fatty liver disease. On the contrary, a low nut consumption can increase your chances of catching a liver disease.

- Whole grains – Whole grains where you can find in foods such as rye, barley, quinoa, brown rice, amaranth, etc. are packed with dietary fiber which can help you get rid of fat and cholesterol. This is advantageous because whole grains can help reduce your risk of developing nonalcoholic fatty liver disease.
- Pasture-raised eggs – Eggs are an incredible source of nutrients that support the liver. Eggs are also loaded with carotenoid antioxidants like vitamin A and vitamin E and an excellent source for vitamin D and omega 3-fatty acids.
- Honey, maple syrup, and stevia –These are the best alternatives to sugar.

Foods to Avoid for Liver Health

While there are foods, drinks and medicinal herbs that can improve your liver condition, there are several types of foods that can negatively impact your liver and lead to poor general health. Below you will find a list of the worst foods for your liver that you should dramatically limit or remove entirely.

ALCOHOL

The leading cause of liver damage is alcohol. Your liver can only tolerate a certain amount of alcohol, so regular consumption of alcoholic beverages will make your liver go through a hard time to process it which will result in damage to the liver.
When the liver enters your liver, it creates a harmful enzyme known as acetaldehyde which can damage liver cells and cause scarring, as well have negative effects on the stomach lining and brain. In addition, alcohol can lead to dehydration which will drive your liver to find water from other sources of the body. Regular and binge drinking can disrupt your body's metabolism, which can drastically increase your risk of developing alcoholic liver disease. For this reason, it's best to limit or cut out alcohol from your diet entirely.

SUGAR

High consumptions of sugar can intensely harm your liver. Excessive amounts of refined sugar can create a fatty buildup which contributes to liver disease. Some studies suggest that sugar can be just as harmful to the liver as alcohol. Foods to avoid that are high in sugar include:

- Soda
- Candy
- Sports and energy drinks
- Store-bought condiments such as barbecue sauce, salad dressings, ketchup, hot sauce
- Store-bought yogurt
- Granola
- Premade meals and television dinners
- Store-bought fruit juice
- Chocolate milk
- Bottled spaghetti sauce
- Flavored coffees and cream
- Breakfast boxed cereals
- Frozen pizza
- Iced tea

SALT

Overconsumption of salt can result in liver damage. If your body has more salt than it requires, it can make your body keep excess water and cause a fatty build up in your liver. Your body only needs a small amount of sodium. Limit your salt intake to 1 to 2 teaspoons of salt per day.

REFINED CARBOHYDRATES

Refined carbohydrates are highly processed grains which can spike your blood sugar levels. Avoid refined carbs as best as you can. It can be found in:

- Table sugar
- Confectioners' sugar
- Honey
- Agave syrup
- Corn syrup
- Brown sugar
- Maple syrup
- Brown rice syrup
- All kinds of flour
- Fruit juices
- Breakfast cereal
- Instant oatmeal
- White rice
- Polished rice
- Instant rice
- Cornstarch
- Potato starch
- Modified food starch

RED MEAT AND PROCESSED FOODS

High consumption of processed foods and red meat can negatively impact your liver condition and insulin resistance. The research found that people who follow a diet high in red and processed meats have a higher risk of developing non-alcoholic fatty liver disease. The reason is that red meat and processed foods have saturated fats that can cause inflammation. Red meats and processed foods that should be avoided include:

- Beef
- Veal
- Pork
- Bacon

- Lamb
- Mutton
- Goat
- Salami
- Smoked sausage

RAW OYSTERS, MUSSELS AND CLAM FISH

If you are suffering from a liver disorder, diabetes, or a weakened immune system, these foods are a big no-no. Raw oysters, clams and mussels contain bacteria that can seriously damage your liver and make you ill. If you absolutely must eat them, make sure they are thoroughly cooked through.

Chapter 4: FAQs About the Liver Rescue Diet

Welcome to the frequently asked questions section. Below you will find the answers to some of the most asked questions regarding the liver rescue diet.

WHAT ARE SOME SYMPTOMS THAT SUGGESTS I HAVE LIVER DISEASE?

One thing you must know is that some individuals suffering from the liver disease can display no symptoms. The most common symptoms include:

- Fatigue
- Excessive tiredness
- Random itching

More prominent signs of liver disease include:

- Dark urine with strong odor
- Yellow eyes and skin
- Light colored bowels
- GI tract bleeding

HOW MUCH ALCOHOL BEFORE IT DAMAGES MY LIVER?

Alcohol in any quantity can cause damage in the liver. The guidelines for alcohol consumption vary for men and women. Men can metabolize and flush away alcohol more efficiently because of their body size, body fat and specific enzymes. So, men can drink no more than 4 drinks in a single day. And with the same reasons, women should drink no more than 2 drinks in a day.

WHAT ARE OTHER THINGS THAT DAMAGES THE LIVER?

Another prominent agent includes acetaminophen which is the main ingredient in most pain relievers such as Tylenol. If you take more than the recommended doses it can result in serious liver damage or liver failure.

CAN YOU REVERSE LIVER DAMAGE?

The liver is the only organ in the body that can regenerate, with the unique ability to replace damaged tissue with brand new cells. In extreme cases such as Tylenol overdose where 50 percent of your liver cells are killed, the liver will restore back to normal within 30 days.

The problem with liver disease is when your ability to regenerate is hindered by the development of liver scar tissue. This is caused when your liver is damaged that prevents the regeneration of the liver via virus, drugs, alcohol, etc. Once scar tissue arises it can be hard to reverse the complication.

IS MILK GOOD FOR THE LIVER?

According to a 2011 study done on rats, milk and other low-fat dairy products can help protect your liver from harm. This is because dairy is high in whey protein which can shield your liver from dangerous toxins.

ARE LIVER DISEASES GENETICALLY INHERITED?

Not necessarily, but if your family has a history with a liver disease it can increase your risk of developing liver disease. However, the majority of individuals develop a liver disease because of alcohol consumption and other dangerous agents. It's a good idea to schedule an appointment with your primary care doctor to discuss concerns and other questions.

WILL EATING LIVER HELP IMPROVE MY LIVER CONDITION?

Eating liver has always been a false medical theory and remedy on improving liver disease. However, the liver of both humans and animals consists of too many toxins that can do more harm than good. In addition, the enzymes and minerals in an animal's liver are not the same ones that humans require.

Amazing Tips for a Successful Liver Rescue Diet and Other Cautions

Healthy habits can make a huge difference in your success with the liver rescue diet. Try to keep the following dieting practices on a consistent basis. Here you will learn the best tips that will help improve your liver and help you lose weight.

AVOID ALCOHOL OR DRINK IN MODERATION

Alcohol is widely known to damage the liver and carries negative effects for the body. For some people, drinking one can of beer or a glass of wine a day lead to liver problems. Due to its high content of toxins, it is always smart to avoid alcohol or drastically limit your alcoholic intake. Here are some tips you can take to practice safe drinking:

- Consider drinking low-alcohol beverages or swap an alcoholic drink with an alcohol-free one.
- Consider blending your favorite wine with mineral water.
- Consider adding lemon juice or lemon zest to beer.
- Try to avoid situations and places where peer pressure is active such as bars.

If you are going through a tough time quitting, schedule an appointment with your primary doctor about receiving professional treatment.

LOSE EXCESS WEIGHT

You are most likely to develop a non-alcoholic fatty liver disease if you are overweight or suffering from obesity or diabetes. Extra fat in your body can create a build-up in your liver. As a result, your liver may swell. Gradually, it can harden and seriously scar liver tissue which is known as cirrhosis. Your best way of prevention is to lose excess weight through diets and exercise.

BE CAREFUL WITH TYLENOL

If you are experiencing pain from a sore back, headache or a cold you might often turn to a pain reliever such as Tylenol – but you need to be careful. Your liver is responsible for processing the drug into safe building blocks that are eventually extracted from the body via urine. However, a tiny amount of Tylenol gets metabolized into a dangerous by-product known as NAPQI. If you take Tylenol by the right amount, your body can swiftly remove the by-product through your urine. However, too much Tylenol means you are producing too much of the dangerous NAPQI that will start harming your liver cells.

DRINK MUCH WATER

Drinking water is the best thing you can do to help your liver and overall health. Water can help cleanse your body from toxins. Your liver is mainly responsible for removing these toxins and drinking your water can help with this process. Staying well hydrated can also help you stay alert, productive, and improve your mood. It recommends drinking up to 3 to 4 liters of water per day in order to help achieve better liver health.

EXERCISE REGULARLY

According to numerous studies, a sedentary lifestyle and fatty liver disease are linked in which you can avoid liver damage with physical activity. Getting enough exercise on a daily schedule can lessen the magnitude of harmful liver diseases. You necessarily do not need to subscribe to a gym membership in order to get regular exercise. A simple 30-minute walk or jog around your neighborhood will suffice. Be consistent in your workout regime. Most of the time people exercise in the first month then gradually quit afterward. Working out with a friend or have a personal trainer who monitors your progress can help keep you right on track.

ALWAYS HAVE SAFE SEX

Engaging in an unprotected safe with numerous partners can negatively impact your liver health. One major risk is that you could sexually transmit hepatitis, a deadly liver disease. To keep your liver and overall health protected from such danger, it's important to use protection every single time.

HAVE GOOD PERSONAL HYGIENE

Keeping good personal hygiene habits such as washing your hands and brushing your teeth will surely help in preventing hepatitis A virus, a liver disease. It's crucial to wash your hands after using the bathroom and changing a baby's diaper. You also should wash your hands before touching your meals. And remember to drink clean water. It's also imperative that you don't use other people's personal hygiene products as it can transfer bacteria and germs.

Chapter 5: Savory Liver Rescue Diet Recipes

Chicken and Poultry Recipes

Salsa Chicken

Time: 45 minutes
Servings: 4

Ingredients:

- 4 boneless, skinless chicken breasts, halved
- 4 teaspoons of taco seasoning mix
- 2 cups of salsa
- 1 cup of cheddar cheese, shredded
- 2 tablespoons of organic sour cream

Instructions:

1. Preheat your oven to 375 degrees Fahrenheit.
2. Season the chicken breasts with the taco seasoning.
3. Grease a baking dish with nonstick cooking spray.
4. Place the chicken breast onto the baking dish and pour the salsa over.
5. Place inside your oven and bake for 25 to 35 minutes or until the chicken is thoroughly cooked through.
6. Sprinkle with the shredded cheddar cheese and return to your oven. Bake until the cheese has melted.
7. Garnish with sour cream.
8. Serve and enjoy!

Nutritional information per serving:

- Calories: 289
- Total Fat: 13.2g
- Total Carbohydrate: 7.8g
- Dietary Fiber: 1.92g
- Protein: 36g

Baked Hawaiian Chicken Kabobs

Time: 40 minutes
Servings: 4

Ingredients:

- 2 pounds of boneless, skinless chicken breasts, cut into thick-sized pieces
- 2 green, yellow or red bell pepper, cut into medium to large sized pieces
- 1 large red onion, cut into pieces
- 1 pineapple, cut into bite-sized chunks

Marinade Ingredients:

- 1 (8-ounce) can of crushed pineapple
- 2 large garlic cloves, crushed or finely minced
- 1/2 cup of low-sodium soy sauce
- 1/3 cup of extra-virgin olive oil
- 1/3 cup of homemade or low-sugar ketchup

Instructions:

1. In a bowl, add the crushed pineapple, crushed garlic, soy sauce, extra-virgin olive oil, and ketchup. Mix until well combined. Reserve 1 cup of the marinade for later.
2. In a large Ziploc bag, add the remaining Ziploc bag along with the chicken. Allow to marinate for up to 2 hours inside your refrigerator.
3. Preheat your oven to 450 degrees Fahrenheit and line a baking sheet with foil.
4. Lay a backing rack over the sheet of foil and generously spray with non-stick cooking spray.
5. Assemble the kebabs with the marinated chicken, pineapple, onions, and peppers. Place onto the backing rack.
6. Place the kabobs inside your oven and bake for 26 minutes, flipping after 15 minutes.
7. Meanwhile, in a saucepan over medium-heat, add the reserved marinade. Bring the mixture to a boil while stirring consistently for 6 to 8 minutes. Remove and set aside.
8. Switch the oven to broil and brush your kabobs with the saucepan marinade. Broil for 5 minutes. Remove the kabobs and allow to cool for 5 minutes. Serve and enjoy!

Nutritional information per serving:

- Calories: 580
- Total Fat: 24g
- Total Carbohydrate: 21.4g
- Dietary Fiber: 2.5g
- Protein: 69.4g

Greek Chicken Pasta

Time: 30 minutes
Servings: 6

Ingredients:

- 1-1/2 pound of boneless, skinless chicken breasts, cut into 1-inch pieces
- 6-ounces of rigatoni pasta
- 1 tablespoon of extra-virgin olive oil
- 1 small yellow onion, finely chopped
- 5 medium garlic cloves, finely minced or crushed
- 2 tablespoons of tomato paste
- 1 cup of homemade low-sodium chicken stock or potassium broth
- 1/2 cup of sun-dried tomatoes, sliced
- 1/2 cup of feta cheese, crumbled
- 1 teaspoon of fine sea salt
- 1 teaspoon of freshly cracked black pepper
- 1/2 teaspoon of onion powder
- 3 tablespoons of fresh parsley, finely chopped
- 1/2 cup of fresh cherry tomatoes, halved
- 1/3 cup of Kalamata olives, halved
- 3/4 cups of heavy cream

Instructions:

1. Prepare your pasta: Cook the rigatoni pasta by following the instructions on the box until al dente.
2. Season the chicken with sea salt, freshly cracked black pepper and onion powder.
3. In a nonstick pan over medium-high heat, add 1 tablespoon of extra-virgin olive oil.
4. Once hot, add the onions and cook for 4 to 6 minutes, stirring occasionally.
5. Add the minced garlic and cook for an additional minute, stirring occasionally.
6. Add the seasoned chicken pieces to the nonstick pan and cook for 6 minutes, flipping once.
7. Add the tomato paste and chicken stock. Allow to simmer for 2 minutes.
8. Add the freshly squeezed lime juice, sun-dried tomatoes, half of the crumbled feta cheese along with 2 tablespoons of fresh parsley. Allow to simmer for 3 minutes.
9. Add the cherry tomatoes, pitted kalamata olives, and heavy cream. Sauté for another 2 minutes.
10. Fold in the rigatoni pasta and sprinkle with the remaining crumbled feta cheese and fresh parsley. Serve and enjoy!

Nutritional information per serving:

- Calories: 957
- Total Fat: 49g
- Total Carbohydrate: 34.1g
- Dietary Fiber: 3.1g
- Protein: 97.2g

Chicken with Mushroom Sauce

Time: 35 minutes
Servings: 4

Ingredients:

- 4 (6-ounce) boneless, skinless chicken breasts halves
- 2 tablespoons of extra-virgin olive oil
- 1/2 teaspoon of fine sea salt
- 1/4 teaspoon of freshly cracked black pepper
- 1/4 cup of shallots, finely chopped
- 1 cup of brown or white mushrooms, sliced
- 2 medium garlic cloves, finely minced or crushed
- 1/2 cup of dry white wine
- 1-1/2 teaspoon of almond flour or coconut flour
- 3/4 cups of homemade low-sodium chicken stock
- 2 tablespoons of butter
- 1 teaspoon of fresh thyme, minced

Instructions:

1. Wrap each chicken breast with plastic wrap and pound using a meat mallet until becomes ½-inch thick.
2. Season the chicken with sea salt and freshly cracked black pepper.
3. In a large nonstick skillet over medium-high heat, add the extra-virgin olive oil.
4. Once hot, add the chicken and cook for 3 minutes per side or until thoroughly cooked. Place the chicken onto a plate and set aside.
5. Add the chopped shallots and sliced mushrooms to the skillet. Cook for 3 to 5 minutes or until brown, stirring occasionally.
6. Add the minced garlic and cook for 1 minute, stirring occasionally.
7. Deglaze the skillet by pouring in the dry white wine. Bring to a boil until most of the wine evaporates.
8. Sprinkle with the 1-1/2 teaspoon of almond flour. Cook for 30 seconds while stirring constantly.
9. Add in the chicken stock and bring to a boil. Allow to cook until thick, stirring occasionally.
10. Stir in the butter and fresh thyme.
11. Ladle the mushroom sauce onto the chicken. Serve and enjoy!

Nutritional information per serving:

- Calories: 295
- Total Fat: 11g
- Total Carbohydrate: 6g
- Dietary Fiber: 1g
- Protein: 20g

Chicken Fajitas

Time: 30 minutes
Servings: 4

Ingredients:

- 3 boneless, skinless chicken breasts, cut into strips
- 1 medium yellow or white onion, sliced
- 1 medium lime, juice
- 3 yellow, green, orange, or red bell peppers, sliced
- 3 tablespoons of extra-virgin olive oil, divided
- 1 teaspoon of organic chili powder
- 1/2 teaspoon of smoked or regular paprika
- 1/2 teaspoon of onion powder
- 1/2 teaspoon of freshly cracked black pepper
- 1/2 teaspoon of organic ground cumin
- 1/2 teaspoon of fine sea salt

Instructions:

1. In a bowl, add 1 tablespoon of extra-virgin olive oil, freshly squeezed lime juice, 1 teaspoon of chili powder, 1/2 teaspoon of smoked paprika, 1/2 teaspoon of onion powder, 1/2 teaspoon of black pepper, 1/2 teaspoon of ground cumin, and fin sea salt. Mix well.
2. Toss the chicken strips with the seasoning mixture.
3. In a skillet over medium-high heat, add 1 tablespoon of extra-virgin olive oil.
4. Working in batches, add the chicken strips and cook for 5 minutes or until thoroughly cooked. Remove and set aside.
5. Add another tablespoon of extra-virgin olive oil to the skillet.
6. Once hot, add the sliced onions and sliced peppers. Cook for 4 minutes or until tender, stirring occasionally.
7. Add the chicken strips to the skillet and continue to cook for a little bit more. Stir until well combined.
8. Serve and enjoy!

Nutritional information per serving:

- Calories: 336
- Total Fat: 16g
- Total Carbohydrate: 11g
- Dietary Fiber: 4g
- Protein: 38g

Coconut Chicken Fingers

Time: 30 minutes
Servings: 6

Ingredients:

- 4 (6-ounce) boneless, skinless chicken breasts, cut into fingers
- 1/2 teaspoon of fine sea salt
- 1/4 teaspoon of freshly cracked black pepper
- 1 cup of almond flour or coconut flour
- 1 large organic egg
- 1 cup of buttermilk
- 1-1/2 cup of unsweetened coconut flakes
- 3 tablespoons of extra-virgin olive oil

Instructions:

1. Season the chicken with fine sea salt and freshly cracked black pepper.
2. In a shallow dish, add the flour.
3. In another shallow dish, add the buttermilk and egg. Mix until well combined.
4. In a third shallow dish, add the coconut flakes.
5. Coat the chicken into the flour and shake.
6. Dip the coated chicken into the egg mixture and finally coat with the coconut flakes.
7. In a large skillet over medium-high heat, add the extra-virgin olive oil.
8. Once the oil is hot, add the chicken and cook for 6 minutes or until brown.
9. Serve and enjoy!

Nutritional information per serving:

- Calories: 210
- Total Fat: 13g
- Total Carbohydrate: 16g
- Dietary Fiber: 2g
- Protein: 29g

Chicken Creole

Time: 30 minutes
Servings: 8

Ingredients:

- 1-1/2 pound of boneless, skinless chicken, cooked and cut into cubes
- 1 cup of celery, sliced
- 1 cup of green peppers, chopped
- 1 cup of white or yellow onions, finely chopped
- 2 medium garlic cloves, finely minced or crushed
- 2 (6-ounce) cans of tomato paste
- 5 cups of homemade low-sodium chicken broth or stock
- 1/4 cup of extra-virgin olive oil
- 1/4 cup of fresh parsley, chopped
- 4 teaspoons of Worcestershire sauce
- 2 teaspoons of fresh lemon juice
- 1 teaspoon of fine sea salt
- 1/2 teaspoon of freshly cracked black pepper
- 1/2 teaspoon of dried thyme

Instructions:

1. In a large nonstick skillet over medium-high heat, add a little bit of

the extra-virgin olive oil.

2. Once the oil is hot and ready, add the chopped celery, chopped green pepper, and chopped onion. Sauté until tender.
3. Add the minced garlic and sauté for 1 minute, stirring occasionally.
4. Add in the flour and cook for 5 minutes or until the flower turns brown, stirring occasionally
5. Stir in the 5 cups of chicken broth and bring to a boil. Cook through for 2 minutes.
6. Add the remaining ingredients and reduce to a simmer. Allow cooking for 10 minutes. Adjust the seasoning if necessary.
7. Serve and enjoy!

Nutritional information per serving:

- Calories: 271
- Total Fat: 13g
- Total Carbohydrate: 9g
- Dietary Fiber: 2g
- Protein: 28g

Baked Lemon Pepper Chicken

Time: 35 minutes
Servings: 4

Ingredients:

- 4 boneless, skinless chicken breasts
- 1/4 cup of freshly squeezed lemon juice
- 2 tablespoon of extra-virgin olive oil
- 4 teaspoons of organic lemon pepper
- 2 teaspoons of dried oregano
- 2 teaspoons of dried basil
- 1 teaspoon of fine sea salt

Instructions:

1. Preheat your oven to 350 degrees Fahrenheit.
2. Grease a baking dish with non-stick cooking spray
3. Place the chicken breasts onto your baking dish.
4. Drizzle the freshly squeezed lemon juice along with the extra-virgin olive oil.
5. In a bowl, add the organic lemon pepper, dried oregano, dried basil, and fine sea salt. Stir until well combined.
6. Place the baking dish inside your oven and bake for 30 minutes or until the chicken is tender and thoroughly cooked.
7. Serve and enjoy!

Nutritional information per serving:

- Calories: 178
- Total Fat: 7g
- Total Carbohydrate: 5g
- Dietary Fiber: 1g
- Protein: 25g

Slow Cooker Cilantro Lime Chicken

Time: 4 hours and 30 minutes
Servings: 6

Ingredients:

- 3 pounds of boneless, skinless chicken breasts, halves
- 1 (16-ounce) jar of salsa
- 1 (1.25-ounce) package of dry taco seasoning mix
- 1/2 teaspoon of fine sea salt
- 1/2 teaspoon of freshly cracked black pepper
- 1 medium lime, juiced
- 3 tablespoons of fresh cilantro, finely chopped

Ingredients:

1. Add the jar of salsa, dry taco seasoning mix, lime juice, and fresh cilantro into your slow cooker. Stir until well combined.
2. Place the chicken breasts and stir until the chicken is well coated with the salsa.
3. Cover with a lid and cook on "High" setting for 4 hours.
4. Transfer the chicken to a cutting board and shred using two forks. Return to your slow cooker and stir well into the salsa.
5. Serve and enjoy!

Nutritional information per serving:

- Calories: 273
- Total Fat: 4.8g
- Total Carbohydrate: 9.6g
- Dietary Fiber: 3.1g
- Protein: 45.2g

Soy Sauce and Garlic Marinated Chicken

Time: 45 minutes
Servings: 4

Ingredients:

- 4 boneless, skinless chicken breasts
- 2 tablespoons of extra-virgin olive oil
- 4 medium garlic cloves, finely minced or crushed
- 1/2 cup of low-sodium soy sauce
- 1/2 teaspoon of red pepper flakes
- 1/2 teaspoon of freshly cracked black pepper

Instructions:

1. In a large bowl, add the minced garlic cloves, soy sauce, extra-virgin olive oil, red pepper flakes, and freshly cracked black pepper. Mix well.
2. Add the chicken breasts and allow to

marinate for up to 2 hours.

3. Preheat your oven to 425 degrees Fahrenheit and line a baking pan with aluminum foil.
4. Place the chicken breasts onto the baking pan and place inside your oven. Bake for 40 minutes or until the chicken is thoroughly cooked and tender.
5. Serve and enjoy!

Nutritional information per serving:

- Calories: 323
- Total Fat: 32g
- Total Carbohydrate: 21g
- Dietary Fiber: 3g
- Protein: 39g

Fish and Seafood Recipes

Baked Salmon

Time: 25 minutes
Servings: 5

Ingredients:

- 1-1/2 pound of wild-caught salmon fillets, skinless or skin-on
- 1 tablespoon of extra-virgin olive oil or coconut oil, melted
- 2 tablespoons of unsalted or salted butter
- 1 large garlic clove, peeled and crushed
- 1 tablespoon of freshly squeezed lemon juice
- 2 tablespoons of fresh parsley, finely chopped
- 1/2 teaspoon of fine sea salt
- 1/2 teaspoon of freshly cracked black pepper

Instructions:

1. Preheat your oven to 375 degrees Fahrenheit.
2. Line a baking sheet with parchment paper.
3. Add the salmon fillets onto the baking sheet.
4. Drizzle with the olive oil. Sprinkle with fine sea salt and freshly cracked black pepper.
5. Place inside your oven and bake for 20 minutes.
6. In a bowl, add the 2 tablespoons of melted butter, lemon juice, crushed garlic, and fresh parsley. Mix well.
7. Brush the butter mixture generously over the salmon fillets.
8. Serve and enjoy!

Nutritional information per serving:

- Calories: 248
- Total Fat: 14g
- Total Carbohydrate: 0.5g
- Dietary Fiber: 0g
- Protein: 31g

Salmon Burger

Time: 50 minutes
Servings: 10

Ingredients:

- 2 pounds of wild-caught salmon fillets, cut into cubes
- 1 medium red or yellow onion, finely

chopped

- 2 large garlic cloves, crushed
- 1/2 cups of red lentils, cooked
- 1 large pasture-raised egg,
- 2 tablespoons of Dijon mustard
- 3 tablespoons of fresh parsley, minced
- 1 teaspoon of fine sea salt
- 1/2 teaspoon of freshly cracked black pepper
- 2 tablespoons of coconut oil, melted
- 3/4 cups of water
- Whole wheat buns or lettuce leaves (for serving)
- Tomato slices (for serving)
- Lettuce leaves (for serving)
- Mayonnaise (for serving)

Instructions:

1. Prepare your lentils: In a small pot, add the 1/2 cups of red lentils and 3/4 cups of water. Bring to a boil and reduce the heat. Allow to simmer for 10 minutes. Remove the pot from the heat and set aside.
2. On a cutting board, use a sharp knife to mince the salmon fillets until resembles a finely chopped texture. Alternatively, you can use a food processor.
3. Transfer the finely minced salmon to a large bowl.
4. Add the cooked lentils, onion, garlic, egg, Dijon mustard, fresh parsley, sea salt, and freshly cracked black pepper. Stir until well combined together.
5. Form 10 patties with the salmon mixture.
6. In a large nonstick skillet over medium-high heat, add the coconut oil.
7. Once the oil is hot, add the salmon patties to the skillet. Cook for 5 minutes or until the edges turn white. Flip and cook for an additional 5 minutes. Continue this process until all the patties are cooked.
8. Serve the patty on hamburger buns or lettuce leaves along with optional toppings.
9. Enjoy!

Nutritional information per serving:

- Calories: 198
- Total Fat: 8g
- Total Carbohydrate: 8g
- Dietary Fiber: 1g
- Protein: 22gSalmon Stir-Fry

Salmon Stir-Fry

Time: 20 minutes
Servings: 4

Ingredients:

- 1-1/2 pound of salmon fillets, cut into 1-inch pieces

- 2 cups of green beans, trimmed and coarsely chopped
- 3 tablespoons of low-sodium soy sauce
- 2 cups of button mushrooms, sliced
- 1 medium garlic clove, peeled and crushed
- inch piece of fresh ginger, peeled and minced
- 2 teaspoons of toasted sesame oil, divided
- 1 to 2 tablespoons of freshly squeezed lemon juice
- 1/4 cup of green onions, chopped (optional)
- 1/2 tablespoon of toasted sesame seeds (optional)

Instructions:

1. In a bowl, add the salmon pieces and 2 tablespoons of soy sauce. Cover with plastic wrap and place inside your refrigerator. Allow to marinate for 2 hours or overnight.
2. In a large nonstick skillet over medium heat, add 1 teaspoon of sesame oil.
3. Once the oil is hot and ready, add the salmon cubes, minced garlic, and minced ginger. Cook for 6 to 9 minutes or until thoroughly cooked, stirring occasionally.
4. Transfer the contents to a bowl and set aside.
5. Raise the heat to medium-high and add the remaining teaspoon of sesame oil.
6. Add in the mushrooms, green beans, and soy sauce. Sauté for 5 minutes, stirring occasionally.
7. Return the salmon contents to the skillet along with the freshly squeezed lemon juice, green onions, and sesame seeds. Give a good stir.
8. Serve and enjoy!

Nutritional information per serving:

- Calories: 206
- Total Fat: 8.3g
- Total Carbohydrate: 9g
- Dietary Fiber: 1g
- Protein: 29g

Lemon and Garlicky Cod Fish

Time: 20 minutes
Servings: 4

Ingredients:

- 4 (6-ounce) cod fish fillets, with skin or without skin
- 2 teaspoons of unsalted butter
- 2 medium garlic cloves, crushed
- 2 tablespoons of freshly squeezed lemon juice
- 2 tablespoons of fresh parsley, finely chopped

- 1 tablespoon of extra-virgin olive oil, coconut oil or avocado oil
- 1/2 teaspoon of fine sea salt
- 1/2 teaspoon of freshly cracked black pepper

Instructions:

1. Preheat your oven to 400 degrees Fahrenheit.
2. Grease a large baking dish with nonstick cooking spray.
3. Place the cod pieces onto the baking dish and season with fine sea salt and freshly cracked black pepper.
4. In a nonstick skillet over medium-low heat, add the 2 teaspoons of unsalted butter and 1 tablespoon of extra-virgin olive oil.
5. Once hot, add the garlic and cook for 1 minute, stirring occasionally.
6. Stir in the freshly squeezed lemon juice and freshly chopped parsley. Remove from the heat.
7. Generously drizzle the garlic-lemon mixture over the cod fish fillets.
8. Place the baking dish inside your oven and bake for 10 to 15 minutes or until the cod is thoroughly cooked.
9. Serve and enjoy!

Nutritional information per serving:

- Calories: 271
- Total Fat: 8g
- Total Carbohydrate: 13g
- Dietary Fiber: 1g
- Protein: 39g

England Fish Pie

Time: 30 minutes
Servings: 4

Ingredients:

- 1 cup of homemade low-sodium fish stock
- 1 cup of low-fat dairy milk
- 12-ounces of salmon fillets or other fatty fish, cut into bite-sized pieces
- 1 bay leaf
- 1/4 cup of butter
- 1/4 cup of almond flour
- 1 tablespoon of fresh parsley, finely chopped
- 1 medium leek, washed thoroughly and finely sliced (using only the white parts)
- 5-1/2 cups of mashed potatoes
- 1/2 teaspoon of fine sea salt
- 1/2 teaspoon of freshly cracked black pepper

Instructions:

1. Preheat your oven to 355 degrees Fahrenheit.

2. In a large saucepan, add the fish stock and bring to a boil. Once it reaches a boil, reduce the heat to a simmer.
3. Add the salmon pieces, bay leaf and simmer for 5 minutes.
4. Using a slotted spoon, remove the salmon pieces and reserve the fish stock.
5. In a saucepan over medium-high heat, add the butter. Once melted, add the leeks and cook for 5 minutes or until softened, stirring occasionally.
6. Use a whisk or a wooden spoon to stir in the flour.
7. Pour in the fish stock to the saucepan and continue to stir.
8. Bring the mixture to a boil and cook for another 3 minutes or until the liquid has thickened.
9. Remove from the heat and discard the bay leaf. Gently stir in the fish, fresh parsley, sea salt, and freshly cracked black pepper.
10. Transfer the fish and sauce to a baking dish and cover spread a layer of mashed potatoes.
11. Place inside your oven and bake for 23 to 29 minutes or until the sauce begins to bubble from under the layer of mashed potatoes.
12. Serve and enjoy!

Nutritional information per serving:

- Calories: 432
- Total Fat: 22g
- Total Carbohydrate: 48g
- Dietary Fiber: 6g
- Protein: 12g

Grilled Salmon with Avocado Salsa

Time: 10 minutes
Servings: 4

Salmon Ingredients:

- 2 pounds of wild-caught salmon fillets, cut into 4 separated pieces
- 1 tablespoon of extra-virgin olive oil
- 1 teaspoon of fine sea salt
- 1 teaspoon of organic ground cumin
- 1 teaspoon of smoked or regular paprika
- 1 teaspoon of onion powder
- 1/2 teaspoon of ancho chili powder
- 1 teaspoon of freshly cracked black pepper

Avocado Salsa Ingredients:

- 1 or 2 medium-sized avocados, peeled and cut into cubes
- 1/2 medium red onion, thinly sliced or finely chopped

- 2 medium limes, juiced
- 1 tablespoon of fresh cilantro, finely chopped

Instructions:

1. In a small bowl, add the fine sea salt, ground cumin, smoked paprika, onion powder, ancho chili powder, and freshly cracked black pepper. Mix well.
2. Rub each salmon fillet pieces with the seasoning mix and drizzle with 1 tablespoon of extra-virgin olive oil. Refrigerate and allow to marinate for 30 minutes.
3. Preheat your grill.
4. Once the grill is hot and ready, add the salmon pieces and grill for 5 minutes or until thoroughly cooked through.
5. In a bowl, add the avocado cubes, sliced red onion, lime juice, and fresh cilantro. Stir until well combined.
6. Ladle the avocado salsa on top of each salmon pieces.
7. Serve and enjoy!

Nutritional information per serving:

- Calories: 457
- Total Fat: 11g
- Total Carbohydrate: 26g
- Dietary Fiber: 6g
- Protein: 48g

Scallops with Lemon Butter

Time: 15 minutes
Servings: 4

Scallop Ingredients:

- 1 pound of scallops
- 1 tablespoon of coconut oil, melted
- 1/2 teaspoon of fine sea salt
- 1/2 teaspoon of freshly cracked black pepper

Lemon Butter Sauce Ingredients:

- 2 tablespoons of unsalted butter
- 2 medium garlic cloves, peeled and crushed or finely minced
- 2 tablespoons of freshly squeezed lemon juice
- 2 tablespoons of fresh parsley, finely chopped
- A dash of fine sea salt
- A dash of freshly cracked black pepper

Instructions:

1. Season the scallops with fine sea salt and freshly cracked black pepper.
2. In a large skillet over medium-high heat, add 1 tablespoon of coconut oil.
3. Once the coconut oil has melted, working in batches, add the scallops and cook for 2 minutes per side. Remove and set aside.
4. Add 2 tablespoons of unsalted butter to the same skillet. Allow to melt.

5. Once melted, add in the minced garlic and sauté for 1 minute or until mildly fragrant, stirring occasionally.
6. Stir in the freshly squeezed lemon juice. Season with sea salt and freshly cracked black pepper.
7. Drizzle the lemon butter sauce over the scallops. Garnish with fresh parsley.
8. Serve and enjoy!

Nutritional information per serving:

- Calories: 189
- Total Fat: 10g
- Total Carbohydrate: 2g
- Dietary Fiber: 0g
- Protein: 22g

Fish Tacos with Citrus Slaw

Time: 45 minutes
Servings: 4

Fish Tacos Ingredients:

- 1-1/2 pound of salmon or cod, cut into bite-sized pieces
- Sea salt
- Freshly cracked black pepper
- 1/2 teaspoon of organic ground cumin
- 1/2 teaspoon of organic ground coriander
- 2 tablespoons of avocado oil or olive oil
- Corn tortillas (for serving)

Sauce Ingredients:

- 1 cup of mayonnaise
- 1/2 cup of organic sour cream
- 5 medium garlic cloves
- 1 tablespoon of fresh lime or lemon zest
- 1 tablespoon of freshly squeezed lime or lemon juice
- 1/4 teaspoon of organic cayenne pepper
- 1/4 teaspoon of fine sea salt

Slaw Ingredients:

- 2 cups of red cabbage, thinly shredded
- 4 cups of green cabbage, thinly shredded
- 1/4 cup of avocado oil or extra-virgin olive oil
- 1 tablespoon of freshly squeezed lemon juice
- 1/4 cup of freshly squeezed orange juice
- 1 teaspoon of fresh orange zest
- 1/4 cup of fresh cilantro, chopped
- 1 teaspoon of raw honey

Instructions:

1. To make the fish taco sauce: Add the mayonnaise, sour cream, garlic cloves, lime zest, lime juice, cayenne pepper and ¼ teaspoon of fine sea salt to a

food processor. Process until smooth and well blended together. Transfer to a bowl, glass jar or squeeze bottle and set aside.

2. To make the slaw: In a large bowl, add the avocado oil, lemon juice, orange juice, orange zest, and raw honey. Mix until well combined. Gently stir in the shredded red cabbage, green cabbage, and fresh cilantro. Set aside.
3. To make the fish tacos: Season the salmon or cod fish pieces with sea salt, freshly cracked black pepper, ground cumin, and ground coriander.
4. Preheat your oven to 370 degrees Fahrenheit.
5. Line a baking sheet with foil and place the fish pieces on top. Drizzle with the avocado oil.
6. Place inside your oven and bake for 6 to 10 minutes or until thoroughly cooked. Remove from your oven and allow to cool.
7. To assemble your fish tacos: Generously add fish to corn tortillas, top with slaw, and drizzle with the fish sauce.
8. Serve and enjoy!

Nutritional information per serving:

- Calories: 656
- Total Fat: 48.9g
- Total Carbohydrate: 22.6g
- Dietary Fiber: 22.8g
- Protein: 37g

Slow-Roasted Salmon with Fennel, Citrus and Chiles

Time: 1 hour
Servings: 4

Ingredients:

- 2 pounds of wild-caught salmon filets
- 3/4 cups of extra-virgin olive oi
- 4 fresh sprigs of dill
- 1/2 teaspoon of fine sea salt
- 1/2 teaspoon of freshly cracked black pepper
- 1 red chile or jalapeno, thinly sliced
- 1 medium-sized fennel bulb, thinly sliced
- 1 medium lemon, thinly sliced and seeded
- 1 blood orange, thinly sliced and seeded

Instructions:

1. Preheat your oven to 275 degrees Fahrenheit.
2. Season the salmon fillet with sea salt and freshly cracked black pepper.
3. In a baking dish, add the sliced fennel, blood orange slices, lemon slices, sliced chiles and fresh sprigs of dill.
4. Place the salmon fillet on top of the sliced vegetables and fruit. Drizzle with the 3/4 cups of extra-virgin olive

oil.

5. Place inside your oven and roast for 30 to 40 minutes.
6. Transfer the salmon to a serving platter and cut into bite-sized pieces
7. Spoon the fennel-citrus mixture and extra-virgin olive oil over the salmon fillets.
8. Serve and enjoy!

Nutritional information per serving:

- Calories: 487
- Total Fat: 38g
- Total Carbohydrate: 71g
- Dietary Fiber: 8g
- Protein: 4g

Thai-Inspired Salmon

Time: 30 minutes
Servings: 6

Ingredients:

- 6 (6-ounce) wild-caught salmon fillets, with skin or without skin
- 1/2 teaspoon of fine sea salt
- 3 tablespoons of fresh green onions, finely chopped

Thai Sweet Chili Sauce Ingredients:

- 1/2 cup of pure maple syrup or raw honey
- 1/4 cup of filtered water
- 1 small garlic clove, finely grated
- 2 tablespoons of rice vinegar
- 1 tablespoon of cornstarch
- 1/2 teaspoon of red chili pepper flakes
- 1 teaspoon of fine sea salt

Instructions:

- In a saucepan over high heat, add all the ingredients and stir until well blended together.
- Bring the mixture to a boil and reduce the heat. Allow to simmer for 6 to 9 minutes or until thickened, stirring constantly. Remove from the heat and set aside.
- In a baking dish, add the salmon fillets.
- Sprinkle with fine sea salt and top with 1 to 2 tablespoons of the sauce. Allow to marinate for 4 hours or overnight.
- Preheat your broiler and place the baking dish inside.
- Broil the salmon fillets for 8 hours. Remove from your oven and generously brush with the remaining sauce.
- Return the baking dish inside your oven and broil for an additional 4 minutes or until caramelized.
- Garnish with green onions.
- Serve and enjoy!

Nutritional information per serving:

- Calories: 277
- Total Fat: 8g
- Total Carbohydrate: 13g
- Dietary Fiber: 2g
- Protein: 38g

Sweet Potato Chili

Time: 45 minutes
Servings: 4

Ingredients:

- 1 tablespoon of olive oil
- 1 medium red onion, finely chopped
- 2 large sweet potatoes, cut into cubes
- 1 green bell pepper, seeded and chopped
- 4 medium garlic cloves, finely minced
- 3 cups of homemade low-sodium vegetable broth
- 1 (28-ounce) can of diced tomatoes, undrained
- 1 (4.5-ounce) can of green chiles, undrained
- 1 (15-ounce) can of kidney beans, drained and rinsed
- 1 (15-ounce) can of black beans, drained and rinsed
- 1 (15-ounce) can of pinto beans, drained and rinsed
- 1 medium lime, juice
- 2 tablespoons of chili powder
- 2 teaspoons of smoked paprika or regular paprika
- 2 teaspoons of organic ground cumin
- 1 teaspoon of dried oregano
- 1/2 teaspoon of seas salt
- 1/2 teaspoon of freshly cracked black pepper

Instructions:

1. In a large pot over medium-high heat, add the 1 tablespoon of olive oil.
2. Once the olive oil is hot and ready, add the chopped onions, cubed sweet potatoes, chopped bell pepper, and minced garlic.
3. Season with sea salt and freshly cracked black pepper. Sauté until the vegetables have softened, typically around 5 to 7 minutes.
4. Add all the seasonings and stir until well coated with the vegetables.
5. Pour in the 3 cups of vegetable broth, diced tomatoes, green chiles, and beans. Bring to a boil and reduce the heat to a simmer.
6. Cover with a lid and allow to simmer for 30 minutes and the chili is thick, stirring occasionally. Squeeze the lime juice. Serve and enjoy!

Nutritional information per serving:

- Calories: 451
- Total Fat: 6.1g
- Total Carbohydrate: 78g
- Dietary Fiber: 27g

- Protein: 22g

Balsamic Beet Burgers

Time: 35 minutes
Servings: 6

Ingredients:

- 1 cup of balsamic vinegar
- 1/4 cup of truvia brown sugar or low-carb alternatives
- 2 tablespoons of extra-virgin olive oil.
- 1/4 cup of whole grained oats
- 1 (15-ounce) can of black beans, drained and rinsed
- 1 large beet, peeled and chopped
- 1 small onion, finely chopped
- 3 medium garlic cloves, minced
- 1/4 cup of fresh dill, chopped
- 1/2 teaspoon of sea salt
- 1/2 teaspoon of freshly cracked black pepper
- 1 tablespoon of extra-virgin olive oil

Serving Ingredients:

- 6 bread buns or lettuce leaves
- Sliced lettuce
- Sliced tomatoes
- Mayonnaise

Instructions:

1. In a small saucepan over medium-high heat, add the balsamic vinegar and truvia brown sugar. Bring to a simmer and allow to simmer for 15 minutes, stirring until thickened.
2. In a food processor, add the oats and blend until resembles flour.
3. Add the black beans, chopped beets, onion, minced garlic, fresh dill, sea salt, freshly cracked black pepper, and 2 tablespoons of the balsamic vinegar mixture. Pulse until smooth.
4. Form the beet mixture into 6 patties.
5. In a skillet over medium-high heat, add 1 tablespoon of extra-virgin olive oil
6. Once hot, add the beets and cook for 4 minutes Drizzle with 1 to 2 teaspoons of balsamic vinegar.
7. Flip and cook for another 4 minutes or until lightly browned.
8. Continue to cook the remaining beet patties.
9. Place the beet patties onto burger buns and lettuce leaves along with desirable toppings.
10. Serve and enjoy!

Nutritional information per serving:

- Calories: 344
- Total Fat: 7.1g
- Total Carbohydrate: 54g
- Dietary Fiber: 8g
- Protein: 11.9g

Vegetable Stir-Fry

Time: 20 minutes
Servings: 2

Ingredients:

- 2 teaspoons of cornstarch
- 1/2 cup of cold water
- 3 tablespoons of low-sodium soy sauce or coconut aminos
- 1 cup of fresh broccoli florets
- 1 medium carrot, thinly sliced
- 1/2 small yellow or white onion, sliced
- 1/2 to 1 cup of brown mushrooms, sliced
- 2 medium garlic cloves, minced
- 1 zucchini, julienned
- 1 cup of cabbage, finely shredded
- 1 tablespoon of extra-virgin olive oil

Instructions:

1. In a bowl, add the 2 teaspoons of cornstarch, 1/2 cup of water and 3 tablespoons of soy sauce.
2. In a large skillet over medium-high heat, add the 1 tablespoon of extra-virgin olive oil.
3. Once the oil is hot and ready, add the broccoli florets, thinly sliced carrots, and sliced onions. Sauté for 5 minutes, stirring occasionally.
4. Add the shredded cabbage, julienned zucchini, sliced mushrooms, and minced garlic. Sauté until the vegetables are tender, stirring frequently.
5. Stir in the cornstarch mixture and continue to cook until begins to thicken.
6. Serve and enjoy!

Nutritional information per serving:

- Calories: 157
- Total Fat: 9g
- Total Carbohydrate: 18g
- Dietary Fiber: 6g
- Protein: 7.3g

Vegetarian Stuffed Pepper

Time: 40 minutes
Servings: 6

Ingredients:

- 6 medium-sized green, red or yellow bell pepper, tops removed and inner portions scooped out
- 2 tablespoons of olive oil, avocado oil, or coconut oil
- 3 medium garlic cloves, crushed
- 1 1/2 pound of ground turkey
- 1 (14.5-ounce) can of diced tomatoes
- 2 teaspoons of Italian seasoning
- 1/2 teaspoon of fine sea salt
- 1/2 teaspoon of freshly cracked black pepper
- 3/4 cups of marinara sauce
- 1/2 cup of cheddar cheese, shredded
- 1/2 cup of mozzarella cheese, shredded

Instructions:

1. Preheat your oven to 375 degrees Fahrenheit.
2. Prepare your bell peppers: Remove the tops of the bell peppers. Use a spoon to scoop out the seeds and hollow out the insides. Brush with 1 tablespoon of olive oil
3. In a medium skillet over medium-high heat, add the remaining tablespoon of olive oil. Once hot, add the crushed garlic and saute for 1 minute or until fragrant.
4. Add the ground turkey to the skillet and cook until no longer pink.
5. Add the can of diced tomatoes and season with Italian seasoning, sea salt, and freshly cracked black pepper. Allow to cook through for 5 minutes, stirring occasionally.
6. Stuff the bell peppers with the ground turkey mixture.
7. Add the marinara sauce to the skillet to combine with the liquid inside. Stir well before adding to a baking dish.
8. Place the bell peppers onto the baking dish and bake for 20 minutes.
9. Serve and enjoy!

Nutrition information per serving:

- Calories: 245
- Total Fat: 15g
- Total Carbohydrate: 11g
- Dietary Fiber: 4g
- Protein: 22g

Vegetarian Gumbo

Time: 50 minutes
Servings: 4

Ingredients:

- 1/2 cup of olive oil or other cooking oils
- 1/3 cup of almond flour
- 1 small onion, finely chopped
- 1 green bell pepper, chopped
- 3 celery stalks, chopped
- 1 (28-ounce) can of diced tomatoes
- 2 cups of fresh green beans, trimmed and cut into bite-sized pieces
- 3 carrots, sliced
- 1 parsnip, diced
- 1 cup of fresh okra, sliced
- 1 tablespoon of organic ground cumin
- 1 tablespoon of smoked paprika or regular paprika
- 1 tablespoon of dried oregano
- 1/4 teaspoon of cayenne pepper
- 4 cups of water

Instructions:

1. In a Dutch oven over medium-high heat, add the olive oil.
2. Once the oil is hot, add the flour and

cook for 10 minutes, stirring occasionally.
3. Add all the chopped vegetables and cook until softened, stirring occasionally.
4. Add the 4 cups of water and bring to a boil. Reduce the heat and allow to simmer for 40 minutes or until the vegetables are tender.
5. Season with fine sea salt and freshly cracked black pepper.
6. Serve and enjoy!

Nutritional information per serving:

- Calories: 219
- Total Fat: 22g
- Total Carbohydrate: 15.1g
- Dietary Fiber: 5g
- Protein: 3g

Vegetable Fajitas

Time: 20 minutes
Servings: 4

Fajita Ingredients:

- 4 portobello mushrooms caps
- 1 large red onion, thinly sliced
- 3 medium-sized bell peppers (green, yellow and red), sliced
- 4 (8-inch) flour tortillas
- 1 tablespoon of extra-virgin olive oil

Mojo Chili Marinade Ingredients:

- 2 teaspoons of fresh orange zest
- 1/2 cup of fresh orange juice
- 1 tablespoon of freshly squeezed lime juice
- 1/3 cup of extra-virgin olive oil
- 1 tablespoon of chili powder
- 1 tablespoon of crushed garlic
- 2 tablespoons of crushed onion
- 1/4 teaspoon of fine sea salt
- 1/4 teaspoon of freshly cracked black pepper

Instructions:

1. To prepare the mojo chili marinade ingredients: In a food processor, add all the ingredients and pulse until smooth.
2. In a large bowl, add the vegetables along with the marinade. Stir until well coated.
3. Place inside your bowl and allow to marinate for up to 2 hours.
4. In a large skillet over medium-high heat, add 1 tablespoon of extra-virgin olive oil.
5. Add the vegetable and cook for 5 to 10 minutes or until the vegetables are tender, stirring occasionally.
6. Spoon the vegetables to the tortillas.
7. Serve and enjoy!

Nutritional information per serving:

- Calories: 275
- Total Fat: 17.8g
- Total Carbohydrate: 27.4g
- Dietary Fiber: 4.7g
- Protein: 5.9g

Cheesy Cauliflower Casserole

Time: 55 minutes
Servings: 8

Ingredients:

- 1 large head of cauliflower, cut into florets
- 1 medium-sized green bell pepper, seeded and diced
- 1 medium-sized red bell pepper, seeded and diced
- 1 cup of mushrooms, sliced
- 1 small onion, finely chopped
- 4 tablespoons of butter, melted
- 1/3 cup of almond flour
- 2 cups of heavy cream
- 1 cup of Asiago cheese or mozzarella cheese, shredded
- 2 to 4 cups of plain croutons (enough to cover the casserole dish)
- 2 tablespoons of parmesan cheese, finely grated
- 1 teaspoon of fine sea salt
- 1/2 teaspoon of freshly cracked black pepper

Instructions:

1. In a large pot over high heat, fill with water and bring to a boil. Add the cauliflower florets and cook for 5 to 10 minutes or until tender. Drain the liquid.
2. Grease a casserole dish with nonstick cooking spray and preheat your oven to 350 degrees Fahrenheit.
3. Place the cauliflower florets onto the casserole dish and set aside.
4. In a large saucepan over medium-high heat, add the 3 tablespoons of butter and allow to melt.
5. Once melted, add the chopped peppers, onions and mushrooms. Sauté for 5 to 7 minutes or until tender, stirring occasionally.
6. Add the almond flour to the saucepan and stir until well combined.
7. Gradually whisk in the heavy cream, stirring constantly. Reduce the heat and allow the sauce to thicken.
8. Add 3/4 cups of the shredded asiago cheese along with salt and black pepper.
9. Transfer the mixture to the cauliflower mixture and cover with foil.
10. Place inside your oven and bake for 20 minutes.
11. Carefully remove the casserole dish from your oven. Spread the croutons,

parmesan cheese, and remaining shredded asiago cheese. Drizzle with the remaining tablespoon of butter.

12. Return to your oven and bake for another 10 to 15 minutes or until the cheese has melted. Serve and enjoy!

Nutritional information per serving:

- Calories: 296
- Total Fat: 20.8g
- Total Carbohydrate: 21.4g
- Dietary Fiber: 4.2g
- Protein: 8.7g

Creamy Spinach and Avocado Zoodles

Time: 25 minutes
Servings: 4

Ingredients:

- 3 medium zucchinis, spiralized
- 1 tablespoon of olive oil
- 1 tablespoon of butter
- 1 whole garlic clove
- 1 medium avocado, peeled and seeded
- 1 cup of fresh spinach
- 1/4 cup of fresh basil
- 1/2 teaspoon of fine sea salt
- 1/2 teaspoon of freshly cracked black pepper
- 1 tablespoon of freshly squeezed lemon juice
- 1/4 cup of parmesan cheese, finely grated
- 1/2 cup of pecans, toasted and finely chopped

Instructions:

1. In a blender, add the whole garlic clove, avocado, fresh spinach, fresh basil, fine sea salt, freshly cracked black pepper, and lemon juice. Pulse until smooth.
2. In a medium skillet over medium-low heat, add 1 tablespoon of olive oil and 1 tablespoon of butter.
3. Add the spiralized zucchini and allow to cook until almost tender. Be careful not to overcook the zucchini.
4. Add the avocado sauce to the spiralized zucchini. Stir until well combined. Continue to cook until well heated through.
5. Top with grated parmesan cheese and finely chopped pecan
6. Serve and enjoy!

Nutritional information per serving:

- Calories: 375
- Total Fat: 34.5g
- Total Carbohydrate: 13.1g
- Dietary Fiber: 7.4g
- Protein: 9.8g

Roasted Butternut Squash Pasta

Time: 1 hour
Servings: 4

Ingredients:

- 1 (8-ounce) package of pasta
- 2 pounds of butternut squash, cut into 1/2-inch cubes
- 2 garlic cloves, peeled
- 1 tablespoon of extra-virgin olive oil
- 1 cup of cauliflower florets
- 2 tablespoons of cream cheese, softened
- 1 cup of unsweetened almond milk or unsweetened coconut milk
- 1/2 cup of frozen peas
- 1/2 teaspoon of fine sea salt
- 1/2 teaspoon of freshly cracked black pepper

Instructions:

1. Preheat your oven to 400 degrees Fahrenheit.
2. Line a baking sheet with parchment paper and spread the butternut squash cubes.
3. Season with sea salt and freshly cracked black pepper and drizzle with extra-virgin olive oil.
4. Add the unpeeled garlic clove to the baking sheet. Place inside your oven and bake for 20 to 30 minutes or until tender. Remove from your oven and allow to cool.
5. In a large pot, cook your pasta according to the package directions. Drain and return to the pot.
6. In a food processor, add the roasted butternut squash, garlic clove, cream cheese, and almond milk. Process until smooth.
7. Add the sauce to the pasta along with the peas. Stir until well combined. Allow the sauce to heat through along with the pasta.
8. Serve and enjoy!

Nutritional information per serving:

- Calories: 339
- Total Fat: 8g
- Total Carbohydrate: 65.9g
- Dietary Fiber: 5.2g
- Protein: 8.1g

Parmesan Eggplant

Time: 1 hour and 30 minutes
Servings: 6

Ingredients:

- 2 large eggplants, cut into 1-inch slices
- 1 tablespoon of extra-virgin olive oil
- 1 large yellow onion, finely chopped
- 2 medium-sized green or red bell peppers, chopped
- 1 large carrot, chopped
- 2 medium garlic cloves, crushed
- 2 tablespoons of tomato paste
- 2 cups of panko breadcrumbs
- 1 teaspoon of dried oregano
- 1/2 cup of almond milk
- 1 (28-ounce) can of crushed tomatoes
- 1 teaspoon of fine sea salt
- 3 cups of mozzarella cheese, shredded
- 1/4 cup of feta cheese, crumbled

Instructions:

1. In a large pot over medium-high heat, add 1 tablespoon of extra-virgin olive oil.
2. Once the oil is hot and ready, add the chopped onions. Cook for 6 minutes or until translucent, stirring occasionally.
3. Add the chopped bell peppers, chopped carrots, and crushed garlic. Cook for 6 to 8 minutes or until softened, stirring occasionally
4. Add 2 tablespoons of tomato paste, 1 teaspoon of fine sea salt and the dried oregano. Cook for an additional 2 to 3 minutes.
5. Stir in the crushed tomatoes and reduce the heat to a simmer until eggplants are ready.
6. Preheat your oven to 375 degrees and line a baking sheet with parchment paper.
7. In a bowl, add the panko breadcrumbs. In a second bowl, add the almond milk.
8. Dip each eggplant slice into the milk and coat with the panko breadcrumbs. Place onto the baking sheet.
9. Place the baking sheet inside your oven and bake for 20 minutes. Remove and set aside.
10. Spoon a couple of tablespoons of the tomato sauce onto a baking dish.
11. Add a layer of the eggplants on top of the sauce. Cover with half of the tomato sauce and 1-1/2 cup of mozzarella cheese.
12. Add another layer of eggplant and spread the remaining tomato sauce. Sprinkle with the rest of the shredded parmesan cheese.
13. Place the baking sheet inside your oven and bake for 40 minutes.
14. Remove from your oven and allow to cool. Serve and enjoy!

Nutritional information per serving:

- Calories: 441
- Total Fat: 22g
- Total Carbohydrate: 38g
- Dietary Fiber: 8g
- Protein: 27g

Flavorful Vegetable Curry

Time: 1 hour and 15 minutes
Servings: 4

Vegetable Ingredients:

- 2 tablespoons of extra-virgin olive oil
- 1 large yellow or white onion, finely chopped
- 4 medium garlic cloves, crushed
- 1 head of cauliflower, chopped into florets
- 3 medium sweet potatoes, cut into cubes
- 1 cup of frozen peas
- 2 medium-sized tomatoes, finely chopped
- 1 lime, juice and zest
- 4 cups of fresh spinach
- 2 tablespoons of fresh cilantro, choppe
- 1 tablespoon of organic tomato paste
- 1 cup of coconut milk
- 2 cups of homemade low-sodium vegetable broth
- 1 teaspoon of fine sea salt
- 1 teaspoon of organic ground cinnamon
- 1 teaspoon of freshly cracked black pepper
- inch fresh knob of ginger, peeled and grated
- 1 tablespoon of ground coriander
- 1 teaspoon of organic ground cumin
- 1 teaspoon of ground turmeric
- 1/2 teaspoon of organic ground cayenne pepper

Instructions:

1. In a large pot or Dutch oven, add the 2 tablespoons of extra-virgin olive oil.
2. Once hot, add the chopped onions, crushed garlic, and ginger. Cook for 6 minutes or until the onions are translucent, stirring occasionally.
3. Add the ground coriander, ground cumin, turmeric, cayenne pepper, fine sea salt, and freshly cracked black pepper.
4. Add the tomato paste and cook for another 1 minute, stirring occasionally.
5. Stir in the vegetable broth and coconut milk. Bring the mixture to a boil and reduce the heat. Allow to simmer for 10 minutes.
6. Add the cauliflower florets, cubed sweet potatoes, chopped tomatoes,

and frozen peas. Allow to simmer for 20 to 25 minutes or until the vegetables are tender, stirring occasionally.

7. Stir in the fresh lime juice, lime zest, fresh spinach, and fresh cilantro. Cook for 2 minutes or until the spinach has wilted, stirring occasionally.
8. Serve and enjoy!

Nutritional information per serving:

- Calories: 539
- Total Fat: 22.3g
- Total Carbohydrate: 79.9g
- Dietary Fiber: 18.4g
- Protein: 12.4g

Vegan Meatloaf

Time: 1 hour
Servings: 6

Meatloaf Ingredients:

- 2 tablespoons of extra-virgin olive oil
- 1 small onion, finely chopped
- 2 carrots, chopped
- 2 celery stalks, chopped
- 3 medium garlic cloves, crushed
- 2 (15-ounce) cans of chickpeas, drained and rinsed
- 1-1/2 cups of panko breadcrumbs
- 2 tablespoons of low-sodium soy sauce
- 2 tablespoons of Worcestershire sauce
- 3 tablespoons of nutritional yeast
- 2 tablespoons of ground flaxseed
- 1/4 cup of low-sugar homemade ketchup
- 1/2 teaspoon of liquid smoke
- Topping Ingredients:
- 1/3 cup of low-sugar homemade ketchup
- 1 teaspoon of Worcestershire sauce

Instructions:

1. Preheat your oven to 375 degrees Fahrenheit.
2. Line a 9-inch loaf pan with parchment paper and spray with nonstick cooking spray.
3. In a large skillet over medium-high heat, add 2 tablespoons of extra-virgin olive oil.
4. Once hot, add the chopped onions, carrots, celery, and crushed garlic. Sauté for 5 minutes or until softened, stirring occasionally. Remove and set aside.
5. In a large bowl, add the can of chickpeas. Use a potato masher to mash.
6. Add the cooked vegetables and remaining meatloaf ingredients. Stir until well combined.
7. Add the vegetable mixture to the loaf

pan and press down. Cover with aluminum foil and place inside your oven. Bake for around 30 minutes or until the meatloaf is set.

8. In a bowl, add the 1/3 cup of ketchup and 1 teaspoon of Worcestershire sauce. Mix well. And spread on top of the meatloaf.
9. Return the loaf pan into your oven and bake for another 15 minutes. Remove from your oven and allow to cool.
10. Serve and enjoy!

Nutritional information per serving:

- Calories: 731
- Total Fat: 15.8g
- Total Carbohydrate: 68.8g
- Dietary Fiber: 28.8g
- Protein: 34.6g

Vegan Enchilada Pasta

Time: 40 minutes
Servings: 6

Ingredients:

- 1 (8-ounce) bag of chickpea pasta
- 2 1/2 cups of red enchilada sauce
- 1 cup of tomatoes, crushed
- 2 cups of homemade low-sodium vegetable stock
- 1 cup of frozen corn
- 1 1/2 cups of black beans, drained and rinsed
- 1 teaspoon of organic chili powder
- 1 teaspoon of organic ground cumin
- 1/2 teaspoon of fine sea salt
- 1/2 teaspoon of freshly cracked black pepper
- 1/2 cup of cheddar cheese, shredded

Topping Ingredients:

- Organic sour cream
- Fresh cilantro
- Diced tomatoes
- Diced jalapenos
- Lime wedges

Instructions:

1. In a bowl, add the black beans and enchilada sauce. Stir until well combined.
2. In a large skillet over high-head, add half of the black bean mixture, 1 cup of crushed tomatoes, 2 cups of vegetable broth, and the bag of chickpea pasta.
3. Bring the mixture to a boil and stir in the corn and remaining black beans.
4. Add the sea salt, chili powder, ground cumin, and freshly cracked black pepper.
5. Cover with a lid and reduce to a simmer. Allow to simmer for 20 minutes, stirring occasionally.

6. Add the shredded cheddar cheese and allow the enchilada pasta to melt.
7. Top with your desired toppings.
8. Serve and enjoy!

Nutrition information per serving:

- Calories: 406
- Total Fat: 5.9g
- Total Carbohydrate: 70.8g
- Dietary Fiber: 16.9g
- Protein: 19.9g

Soups, Stews and Broths Recipes

Cabbage Soup

Time: 25 minutes
Servings: 6

Ingredients:

- 1/2 head of green cabbage, cored and chopped
- 1 cup of celery, finely chopped
- 1 cup of white or yellow onion, finely chopped
- 1 cup of carrots, finely chopped
- 1 green, yellow or red bell pepper, finely chopped
- 3 medium garlic cloves, minced
- 4 cups of homemade low-sodium chicken stock
- 1 (14-ounce) can of diced tomatoes
- 1 teaspoon of dried oregano
- 1 teaspoon of dried basil
- 1/2 teaspoon of crushed red pepper flakes
- 1/2 teaspoon of fine sea salt
- 1/2 teaspoon of freshly cracked black pepper
- 2 tablespoons of extra-virgin olive oil

Instructions:

1. In a large pot over medium-high heat, add 2 tablespoons of extra-virgin olive oil.
2. Once the oil is hot and ready, add the chopped celery, chopped onions, chopped bell peppers, and chopped carrots. Sauté until the vegetables become tender, stirring occasionally.
3. Stir in the minced garlic and sauté for an additional minute.
4. Pour in the 4 cups of chicken stock, diced tomatoes and chopped cabbage.
5. Bring the mixture to a boil. Reduce the heat and allow to simmer until the cabbage becomes tender.
6. Stir in the dried oregano, dried basil, crushed red pepper flakes, freshly cracked black pepper, and fine sea salt.
7. Adjust the seasoning if necessary.
8. Serve and enjoy!

Nutritional information per serving:

- Calories: 100
- Total Fat: 5.3g
- Total Carbohydrate: 12.7g
- Dietary Fiber: 3.7g
- Protein: 2.6g

Homemade Detoxifying Vegetable Broth with Ginger and Turmeric

Time: 1 hour and 30 minutes
Servings: 8

Ingredients:

- 1 gallon of water
- 1 large onion, peeled and coarsely chopped
- 1 leek, coarsely chopped (tops included)
- 4 whole large garlic cloves, peeled
- 3 parsnips, peeled and roughly chopped
- 1 bunch of fresh parsley
- 1/2 head of green cabbage, chopped
- 1 (3-inch) piece of fresh ginger, peeled and chopped
- 3 celery stalks, coarsely chopped
- 1 tablespoon of organic ground turmeric
- 1 teaspoon of fine sea salt

Instructions:

1. In a large stockpot over high heat, add all the ingredients together and give a gentle stir. Bring to a boil and reduce to a simmer.
2. Cover with a lid and allow to simmer for 1 hour and 30 minutes.
3. Once done, strain the liquid using a fine mesh strainer.
4. Discard the vegetables and store the liquid in containers for future use.
5. Serve and enjoy!

Nutritional information per serving:

- Calories: 54
- Total Fat: 0.7g
- Total Carbohydrate: 13g
- Dietary Fiber: 3.9g
- Protein: 2.1g

Bieler's Broth

Time: 20 minutes
Servings: 8 cups

Ingredients:

- 4 medium zucchinis, ends removed and sliced
- 1 pound of green beans, trimmed
- 2 celery stalks, chopped
- 2 bunches of fresh parsley, stemmed
- 4 cups of filtered water

Instructions:

1. In a large pot over high heat, add all the ingredients and give a gentle stir.
2. Bring the mixture to a boil and reduce the heat to a simmer.
3. Cover with a lid and allow to simmer until the vegetables are tender, typically around 15 minutes.
4. Use an immersion blender to puree

the contents until smooth. Alternatively, you can transfer the mixture to a blender and puree in batches.
5. Serve and enjoy!

Nutritional information per serving:

- Calories: 37
- Total Fat: 0.3g
- Total Carbohydrate: 7.5g
- Dietary Fiber: 3.1g
- Protein: 2.3g

Slow-Cooker Lentil Soup

Time: 6 hours
Servings: 8

Ingredients:

- 2 cups of butternut squash, peeled and cut into cubes
- 2 cups of carrots, peeled and sliced
- 2 cups of Yukon potatoes, cubed
- 2 cups of celery, finely chopped
- 1 medium white or yellow onion, finely chopped
- 5 medium garlic cloves, finely minced
- 1 cup of green lentils
- 1 cup of yellow split peas
- 10 cups of homemade low-sodium vegetable or chicken stock
- 2 teaspoons of herbs de provence
- 1 teaspoon of fine sea salt
- 3 cups of kale, stemmed and coarsely chopped
- 1 cup of fresh parsley, chopped
- 1/2 cup of extra-virgin olive oil

Instructions:

1. In a slow-cooker, add the cubed butternut squash, sliced carrots, cubed potatoes, chopped celery, chopped onions, chopped garlic cloves, green lentils, yellow split peas and 10 cups of vegetable stock.
2. Cover with a lid and cook on "High" for 5 to 6 hours.
3. Transfer 4 cups of the soup to a food processor or blender. Blend until smooth and creamy. Return to the slow cooker.
4. Stir in the herbs de provence, fine sea salt, chopped kale, chopped parsley, and extra-virgin olive oil.
5. Serve and enjoy!

Nutritional information per serving:

- Calories: 321
- Total Fat: 15g
- Total Carbohydrate: 40g
- Dietary Fiber: 2g
- Protein: 11g

Roasted Pumpkin and Apple Soup

Time: 1 hour and 10 minutes
Servings: 8

Ingredients:

- 4 pounds of pumpkin, peeled, seeded and cut into cubes
- 4 large apples, cored and cut into eight separate pieces
- 1/4 cup of extra-virgin olive oil
- 1 tablespoon of fresh sage, finely chopped
- 6 cups of homemade low-sodium chicken stock or vegetable stock
- 1 teaspoon of fine sea salt
- 1/2 teaspoon of freshly cracked black pepper

Instructions:

1. Preheat your oven to 450 degrees Fahrenheit.
2. Line a baking sheet with parchment paper and spray with nonstick cooking spray.
3. In a large bowl, add the cubed pumpkin, apples, extra-virgin olive oil, sea salt, and freshly cracked black pepper. Toss until well combined.
4. Transfer the vegetables to a baking sheet and spread. Place inside your oven and bake for 30 minutes.
5. Sprinkle with the fresh sage and continue to bake inside your oven for another 15 to 20 minutes or until brown.
6. Add the roasted vegetables to a large pot along with the 6 cups of chicken stock. Use an immersion blender to puree until smooth. Alternatively, you can work in batches using a blender.
7. Allow the soup to heat through before serving.
8. Enjoy!

Nutritional information per serving:

- Calories: 191
- Total Fat: 10.2g
- Total Carbohydrate: 27g
- Dietary Fiber: 5.9g
- Protein: 4g

Lemon Orzo Soup

Time: 30 minutes
Servings: 6

Ingredients:

- 2 pounds of boneless, skinless chicken breasts or chicken thighs
- 1 (10-ounce) bag of fresh or frozen spinach
- 1 large white, yellow or red onion, finely chopped
- 6 to 8 medium garlic cloves, peeled and minced
- 1 (12-ounce) jar of roasted red peppers

- 1 cup of orzo
- 3 tablespoons of freshly squeezed lemon juice
- 6 cups of homemade low-sodium vegetable or chicken stock

Instructions:

1. In a large pot, add chicken breasts, chicken stock, garlic, and onions. Bring to a boil and boil for 8 to 10 minutes or until the chicken is thoroughly cooked.
2. Transfer the chicken to a cutting board and shred using two forks.
3. Return the shredded chicken to the large pot along with spinach, freshly squeezed lemon juice, orzo, and roasted red peppers.
4. Bring the mixture to a boil and reduce the heat. Allow to simmer until the orzo is cooked through.
5. Serve and enjoy!

Nutritional information per serving:

- Calories: 394
- Total Fat: 6.2g
- Total Carbohydrate: 31.9g
- Dietary Fiber: 3.4g
- Protein: 50.9g

Vegetarian Minestrone Soup

Time: 40 minutes
Servings: 6

Ingredients:

- 1 tablespoon of extra-virgin olive oil
- 1 medium yellow or white onion, finely chopped
- 2 medium garlic cloves, minced
- 1 (28-ounce) can of diced tomatoes
- 1/4 cup of elbow pasta
- 3 cups of water
- 2 medium zucchinis, chopped
- 1 cup of carrots, peeled and sliced
- 1 cup of cannellini beans
- 1 cup of celery, finely chopped
- 2 tablespoons of fresh basil, finely chopped
- 1/2 teaspoon of dried oregano
- 1/2 teaspoon of fine sea salt
- 1/2 teaspoon of freshly cracked black pepper

Instructions:

1. Heat 1 tablespoon of extra-virgin olive oil in a large saucepan over medium-high heat.
2. Once hot and ready, add the onions and sauté for 4 minutes or until lightly browned, typically around 4 to 6 minutes.
3. Add the remaining ingredients except for the elbow pasta. Bring the mixture to a boil.

4. Reduce to a simmer. Allow to simmer for 25 minutes, stirring occasionally.
5. Add the elbow pasta and continue to cook until the pasta is tender. Adjust the seasoning if necessary.
6. Serve and enjoy!

Nutritional information per serving:

- Calories: 89
- Total Fat: 4g
- Total Carbohydrate: 14g
- Dietary Fiber: 4g
- Protein: 3g

Mushroom Soup

Time: 45 minutes
Servings: 4

Ingredients:

- 2 large white onions, finely chopped
- 2 (10-ounce) packages of white button mushrooms, sliced
- 2 (10-ounce) packages of baby portobello mushrooms, sliced
- 20 fresh stalks of thyme, stemmed
- 2 bay leaves
- 1 teaspoon of fine sea salt
- 1 teaspoon of freshly cracked black pepper
- 1 tablespoon of low-sodium soy sauce
- 2 tablespoons of all-purpose flour
- 2 cups of homemade low-sodium vegetable broth
- 2 cups of unsweetened almond milk or unsweetened cashew milk
- 2 tablespoons of extra-virgin olive oil

Instructions:

1. In a saucepan over medium-high heat, add the 2 tablespoons of extra-virgin olive oil.
2. Once the oil is hot and ready, add the chopped onions. Sauté for 5 to 7 minutes, stirring occasionally.
3. Add the sliced white button mushrooms and baby portobello mushrooms. Sauté for 5 minutes, stirring occasionally.
4. Add the fresh thyme and continue to sauté for another 10 minutes or until most of the liquid in mushrooms evaporated.
5. Stir in the fine sea salt, soy sauce, and bay leaf.
6. In a bowl, add the all-purpose flour and vegetable broth. Stir into the mushroom mixture.
7. Stir in the unsweetened almond milk and cook for around 15 minutes, stirring occasionally. Adjust the seasoning if necessary.
8. Serve and enjoy!

Nutritional information per serving:

- Calories: 430
- Total Fat: 36.8g
- Total Carbohydrate: 21.8g

- Dietary Fiber: 5.8g
- Protein: 10.9g

Chicken Liver Detox Soup

Time: 1 hour and 5 minutes
Servings: 8

Ingredients:

- 1-1/2 pound of boneless, skinless chicken breasts
- 8 cups of homemade low-sodium chicken broth or vegetable stock
- 1 large onion, peeled and finely chopped
- 3 cups of broccoli florets
- 2-1/2 cups of carrots, sliced
- 2 cups of celery, chopped
- 1-1/2 cups of frozen peas
- 1/4 cups of fresh parsley, finely chopped
- 3 tablespoons of fresh ginger, peeled and finely grated
- 4 medium garlic cloves, minced
- 2 tablespoons of extra-virgin olive oil
- 1 tablespoon of apple cider vinegar
- 1/2 teaspoon of crushed red pepper
- 1/4 teaspoon of organic ground turmeric
- 1/2 teaspoon of fine sea salt
- 1/2 teaspoon of freshly cracked black pepper

Instructions:

1. In a large sauce pot over medium-high heat, add the extra-virgin olive oil.
2. Once the oil is hot and ready, add the chopped onions, chopped celery, minced ginger, and minced garlic. Sauté for around 6 minutes or until softened, stirring occasionally.
3. Add the chicken, chicken broth, sliced carrots, apple cider vinegar, crushed red pepper, ground turmeric, fine sea salt and freshly cracked black pepper.
4. Bring the mixture to a boil. Reduce the heat and allow to simmer for 20 minutes or until the chicken is thoroughly cooked.
5. Transfer the chicken to a cutting board and shred using two forks.
6. Add the broccoli florets, frozen peas, and fresh parsley to the sauce pot. Allow to simmer until the broccoli has softened.
7. Return the shredded chicken to the soup and adjust the seasoning if necessary.
8. Serve and enjoy!

Nutritional information per serving:

- Calories: 205
- Total Fat: 8g
- Total Carbohydrate: 10.5g
- Dietary Fiber: 4g

- Protein: 23g

The Best Potassium Broth to Cleanse the Liver

Time: 2 to 4 hours
Servings: 16

Ingredients:

- 4 large organic potatoes, well-scrubbed and ONLY using the peels
- 3 large organic carrots, peeled and roughly chopped
- 4 organic celery stalks, chopped
- 3 medium organic beets with green parts included, sliced
- 1 bunch of organic parsley
- 4 quarts of water
- 50 whole garlic cloves
- 2 large onions, peeled and sliced

Instructions:

1. In a large stock pot, add all the vegetables and fill with water. No need to be specific with the amount of water, just ensure that there is enough water.
2. Cover and set on medium-low heat. Allow to simmer for 2 to 4 hours.
3. Strain the vegetables and discard the contents.
4. Refrigerate until ready to serve. Enjoy!

Nutritional information per serving:

- Calories: 71
- Total Fat: 0.2g
- Total Carbohydrate: 16.1g
- Dietary Fiber: 2.6g
- Protein: 2.2g

Appetizers Recipes

Roasted Okra

Time: 35 minutes
Servings: 6

Ingredients:

- 1 pound of okra, tops, and bottom removed, cut into 1/2-inch pieces
- 2 tablespoons of extra-virgin olive oil
- 1 teaspoon of fine sea salt
- 1/2 teaspoon of garlic powder

Instructions:

1. Preheat your oven to 425 degrees Fahrenheit.
2. In a large bowl, add the okra pieces, extra-virgin olive oil, fine sea salt, and freshly cracked black pepper.
3. Line a baking tray with parchment paper and spread the okra evenly.
4. Place inside your oven and bake for 5 to 10 minutes or until tender. Remove from your oven and allow to cool.
5. Serve and enjoy!

Nutritional information per serving:

- Calories: 69
- Total Fat: 4g
- Total Carbohydrate: 6g
- Dietary Fiber: 1.2g
- Protein: 1.1g

Baked Cheddar Cauliflower Bites

Time: 25 minutes
Servings: 4

Ingredients:

- 2 cups of fresh or frozen cauliflower florets
- 1 cup of sharp cheddar cheese, shredded
- 1 large pasture-raised egg, beaten
- 1/4 teaspoon of dried oregano
- 1 medium garlic clove, peeled and minced
- 1/2 teaspoon of fine sea salt
- 1/2 teaspoon of freshly cracked black pepper

Instructions:

1. Preheat your oven to 375 degrees Fahrenheit and grease a muffin tin with nonstick cooking spray.
2. In a microwavable safe bowl, add the cauliflower florets and cover with plastic wrap. Place inside your microwave and microwave for 5 to 9 minutes or until the cauliflower turns

tender.

3. Add the cauliflower to a food processor and pulse until rice-like consistency.
4. Transfer the cauliflower rice to a dishcloth and squeeze out the extra liquid.
5. In a large bowl, add the cauliflower rice, egg, shredded cheddar cheese, dried oregano, sea salt, and freshly cracked black pepper. Stir until well combined.
6. Divide and scoop the cauliflower mixture into the muffin tin.
7. Place the muffin tin inside your oven and bake for 15 minutes or until the edges turn golden brown and the middle is firm. Remove from your oven and allow to cool.
8. Serve and enjoy!

Nutrition information per serving:

- Calories: 153
- Total Fat: 10.38g
- Total Carbohydrate: 4.1g
- Dietary Fiber: 2g
- Protein: 10g

Roasted Brussel Sprouts with Mustard Sauce

Time: 20 minutes
Servings: 6

Ingredients:

- 1-1/2 pound of fresh brussel sprouts, cut in half
- 2 tablespoons of extra-virgin olive oil
- 3 medium garlic cloves, minced

Mustard Sauce Ingredients:

- 1/2 cup of heavy whipping cream
- 3 tablespoons of Dijon mustard
- A small pinch of white pepper
- A small pinch of fine sea salt

Instructions:

1. Preheat your oven to 450 degrees Fahrenheit and grease a baking pan.
2. In a large bowl, add the halved brussel sprouts, minced garlic, and extra-virgin olive oil. Stir until well combined.
3. Transfer the brussel sprouts to the baking pan.
4. Place inside your oven and bake for 10 to 15 minutes or until tender, tossing halfway through.
5. To create the mustard sauce: In a saucepan over medium heat, add the heavy cream, Dijon mustard, white pepper, and fine sea salt. Allow to simmer for 1 minute or until thickens,

stirring occasionally.

6. Spoon the sauce over the roasted brussel sprouts.
7. Serve and enjoy!

Nutritional information per serving:

- Calories: 188
- Total Fat: 13g
- Total Carbohydrate: 14.1g
- Dietary Fiber: 4g
- Protein: 4.1g

Turkey Meatballs with Cranberry Sauce

Time: 35 minutes
Servings: 6

Ingredients:

- 1-1/2 pound of ground turkey
- 1 large egg, beaten
- 1/4 cup of heavy cream
- 1/2 cup of panko breadcrumbs
- 1 tablespoon of extra-virgin olive oil
- 7-ounces of cranberry sauce
- 1/2 cup of orange marmalade
- 1 teaspoon of fine sea salt
- 1 teaspoon of onion powder
- 1/2 teaspoon of Worcestershire sauce
- 1/2 teaspoon of garlic powder
- 1/2 teaspoon of freshly cracked black pepper

Instructions:

1. In a large bowl, add the ground turkey, beaten egg, heavy cream, panko breadcrumb, sea salt, onion powder, Worcestershire sauce, garlic powder, and freshly cracked black pepper. Use your hands to mix until well blended together.
2. Cover with plastic wrap and sit inside your refrigerator for 1 hour.
3. Form meatballs using the turkey meatballs.
4. In a skillet over medium heat, add the extra-virgin olive oil.
5. Once hot and working in batches, add the turkey meatballs and cook until brown. Transfer to plate lined with paper towels.
6. Once all the meatballs are cooked, stir in the orange marmalade and cranberry sauce. Simmer the sauce for 3 minutes.
7. Return the turkey meatballs to the skillet and allow to simmer for 5 minutes.
8. Serve and enjoy!

Nutritional information per serving:

- Calories: 405
- Total Fat: 17.9g
- Total Carbohydrate: 33.3g
- Dietary Fiber: 0.8g
- Protein: 33.4g

- Dietary Fiber: 4g
- Protein: 0.9g

Homemade Guacamole

Servings: 2
Time: 10 minutes

Ingredients:

- 3 medium ripe avocados, skin removed and cubed
- 1 medium garlic clove, minced
- 1/2 teaspoon of fine sea salt
- 1 small onion, finely chopped
- 1/4 cup of mayonnaise
- 2 tablespoons of freshly squeezed lemon juice
- 1 tablespoon of fresh cilantro, chopped
- 2 medium tomatoes, seeded and chopped

Instructions:

1. In a large bowl, add the cubed avocados. Mash with two forks.
2. Mix in the minced garlic, sea salt, chopped onion, mayonnaise, lemon juice, fresh cilantro, and chopped tomatoes.
3. Serve and enjoy!

Nutritional information per serving:

- Calories: 90
- Total Fat: 8g
- Total Carbohydrate: 7g

Cauliflower Hummus

Time: 25 minutes
Servings: 12

Ingredients:

- 3 cups of cauliflower florets
- 5 tablespoons of avocado oil or extra-virgin olive oil
- 1/2 tablespoon of tahini paste
- 3 tablespoons of freshly squeezed lemon juice
- 3 whole garlic cloves
- 2 tablespoons of water
- 1 teaspoon of fine sea salt
- Smoked paprika (for garnishing)

Instructions:

1. In a microwavable safe bowl, add the cauliflower florets, 2 tablespoons of the avocado oil, water, and 3 whole garlic cloves. Microwave for 15 minutes or until tender.
2. In a food processor, add the cauliflower combination, tahini paste, 3 tablespoons of avocado oil, lemon juice, and sea salt. Blend until smooth and adjust the seasoning if necessary.
3. Transfer the hummus to a bowl and sprinkle with smoked paprika.
4. Serve and enjoy!

Nutritional information per serving:

- Calories: 145
- Total Fat: 15g
- Total Carbohydrate: 5g
- Dietary Fiber: 1.2g
- Protein: 2.4g

Spinach and Artichoke Dip

Time: 35 minutes

Servings: 4

Ingredients:

- 1 (14-ounce) can of artichoke hearts, drained and chopped
- 1/2 cup of organic sour cream
- 1/2 cup of organic mayonnaise
- 1 (8-ounce) package of cream cheese, softened
- 1-1/4 cup of parmesan cheese, finely grated
- 1/2 cup of fresh spinach
- 1 medium garlic clove, minced

Instructions:

1. Preheat your oven to 350 degrees Fahrenheit and grease a baking dish.
2. In a large bowl, add the chopped artichoke hearts, sour cream, mayonnaise, softened cream cheese, spinach, 1 cup of grated parmesan cheese, and minced garlic. Stir until well combined.
3. Transfer the artichokes and mixture to the baking dish and top with the remaining 1/4 cup of grated parmesan cheese.
4. Place inside your oven and bake for 20 minutes.
5. Serve and enjoy!

Nutritional information per serving:

- Calories: 511
- Total Fat: 41.8g
- Total Carbohydrate: 21.3g
- Dietary Fiber:
- Protein: 17.9g

Sweet Chili Lime Corn

Time: 15 minutes
Servings: 3

Ingredients:

- 1 (12-ounce) bag of frozen corn
- 2 tablespoons of butter, melted
- 1/2 medium jalapeno, seeded and minced
- 1-1/2 tablespoon of pure raw honey
- 1/8 teaspoon of organic cayenne pepper
- 1 tablespoon of freshly squeezed lime juice
- 1 tablespoon of fresh cilantro, chopped
- 3 tablespoons of Mexican queso fresco, crumbled
- A small pinch of fine sea salt

Instructions:

1. In a cast-iron skillet over medium heat, add the butter.
2. Once hot, add the minced jalapeno and sauté for 1 minute.
3. Add the frozen corn, pure raw honey, cayenne pepper, and fine sea salt. Cook until caramelized, stirring occasionally.
4. Stir in the freshly squeezed lime juice. Top with the fresh cilantro, crumbled Mexican queso fresco and cayenne pepper.
5. Serve and enjoy!

Nutritional information per serving:

- Calories: 398
- Total Fat: 6.9g
- Total Carbohydrate: 85g
- Dietary Fiber: 11g
- Protein: 14g

Mango and Bean Salsa

Time: 30 minutes
Servings: 4

Ingredients:

- 1 mango, peeled and cut into cubes
- 1 cup of dried pinto beans, soaked overnight and drained
- 1/2 to 1 cup of corn kernels
- 1/4 cup of fresh cilantro, chopped
- 2 tablespoons of freshly squeezed lime juice
- 1 medium onion, finely chopped
- 1/2 jalapeno, seeded and diced
- 2 large tomatoes, finely chopped
- 2 tablespoons of olive oil

Instructions:

1. In a large bowl, add all the ingredients and stir until well combined.
2. Serve and enjoy!

Nutritional information per serving:

- Calories: 339

- Total Fat: 8.5g
- Total Carbohydrate: 56.9g
- Dietary Fiber: 11.4g
- Protein: 13.2g

Spicy Roasted Chickpeas

Time: 30 minutes
Servings: 10

Ingredients:

- 2 (15-ounce) cans of chickpeas, drained and rinsed
- 1/2 teaspoon of fine sea salt
- 1/2 teaspoon of organic ground cumin
- 1 teaspoon of organic cayenne pepper
- 2 tablespoons of extra-virgin olive oil

Instructions:

1. Preheat your oven to 400 degrees Fahrenheit and line a baking sheet with parchment paper.
2. In a large bowl, add the chickpeas, fine sea salt, ground cumin, cayenne pepper, and extra-virgin olive oil. Toss until well coated.
3. Add the chickpeas onto the baking sheet and spread evenly.
4. Place inside your oven and bake for 50 to 60 minutes.
5. Remove from your oven and allow to cool.
6. Serve and enjoy!

Nutritional information per serving:

- Calories: 334
- Total Fat: 7.9g
- Total Carbohydrate: 51.6g
- Dietary Fiber: 14.8g
- Protein: 16.4g

Salad Recipes

Roasted Salmon Liver Detox Salad

Time: 20 minutes
Servings: 4

Ingredients:

- 4 (4-ounce) wild-caught salmon fillets
- 1 pound of asparagus, trimmed and cut into 1-1/2-inch pieces
- 2 bunches of fresh watercress
- 1 medium ripe avocado, peeled, cored and sliced
- 1 large English cucumber, thinly sliced
- 1 bunch of beets, thinly sliced
- 1/4 cup of freshly squeezed lemon juice
- 1/4 cup of extra-virgin olive oil
- 1 tablespoon of fresh ginger, finely grated
- 1 tablespoon of Dijon mustard
- 1 medium garlic clove, crushed or finely minced
- A dash of fine sea salt
- A sprinkle of freshly cracked black pepper

Instructions:

1. Preheat your oven to 390 degrees Fahrenheit.
2. Line a baking sheet with parchment paper and place on the salmon fillets.
3. Place the baking sheet inside your oven and bake for 8 to 10 minutes. Remove from the oven and set aside.
4. In a bowl, add the freshly squeezed lemon juice, extra-virgin olive oil, Dijon mustard, crushed garlic, sea salt, and black pepper. Stir until well combined.
5. In a 4 salad bowls, divide and add the watercress, asparagus pieces, cucumber, beet, and avocado.
6. Place a salmon fillet on top of each salad and drizzle with the salad dressing.
7. Serve and enjoy!

Nutritional information per serving:

- Calories: 413
- Total Fat: 29.9g
- Total Carbohydrate: 14.3g
- Dietary Fiber: 6.9g
- Protein: 27g

Greek Kale Salad

Time: 10 minutes

Servings: 4

Salad Ingredients:

- 1 large bunch of kale leaves, torn and finely chopped
- 1 pint of organic cherry tomatoes or grape tomatoes, halved
- 1 medium cucumber, seeded and finely chopped
- 1/2 small red onion, thinly sliced
- 1/2 cup of feta cheese, crumbled

Lemon Dressing Ingredients:

- 1/2 cup of extra-virgin olive oil
- 1/4 cup of freshly squeezed lemon juice
- 1 medium garlic clove, crushed
- 1 teaspoon of dried oregano
- A fine pinch of fine sea salt

Instructions:

1. In a small bowl, add the extra-virgin olive oil, lemon juice, crushed garlic clove, dried oregano, and fine sea salt. Stir until well combined.
2. In a large bowl, add all the salad ingredients and toss until well combined.
3. Drizzle with the lemon olive oil dressing and stir until well combined.
4. Serve and enjoy.

Nutritional information per serving:

- Calories: 319
- Total Fat: 29.5g
- Total Carbohydrate: 12.1g
- Dietary Fiber: 2.3g
- Protein: 5.2g

Mediterranean Herbed Chicken Salad

Time: 25 minutes
Servings: 4

Salad Ingredients:

- 1 pound of boneless, skinless chicken thighs or chicken breasts
- 2 tablespoons of extra-virgin olive oil
- 4 cups of lettuce, washed and chopped
- 1 large English cucumber, finely chopped
- 2 Roma tomatoes, finely chopped
- 1 red onion, sliced
- 1 medium avocado, sliced
- 1/3 cups of Kalamata or black olives, pitted and sliced
- 1 medium lemon, cut into wedges (For serving)

Dressing Ingredients:

- 2 tablespoons of extra-virgin olive oil
- 1/4 cups of freshly squeezed lemon juice
- 2 tablespoons of red wine vinegar

- 2 tablespoons of fresh parsley, chopped
- 2 teaspoons of dried basil
- 2 teaspoons of garlic, minced
- 1 teaspoon of dried oregano
- 1/2 teaspoon of fine sea salt
- 1/4 teaspoon of freshly cracked black pepper

Instructions:

1. In a large bowl, add all the salad dressing ingredients and mix until well combined.
2. In a large dish, add half of the dressing and refrigerate the remaining dressing for later.
3. Place the chicken on the marinade and allow to marinate for up to 2 hours.
4. Meanwhile, in a large salad bowl, add all the salad ingredients and stir until well combined. Set aside for later.
5. In a medium skillet over medium heat, heat 2 tablespoons of extra-virgin olive oil. Once hot, add the chicken and cook on both sides or until browned and thoroughly cooked.
6. Allow the chicken to rest for a few minutes before slicing.
7. Arrange the chicken slices over the salad and drizzle with the dressing.
8. Serve with lemon wedges.

Nutritional information per serving:

- Calories: 338
- Total Fat: 22g
- Total Carbohydrate: 14g
- Dietary Fiber: 7g
- Protein: 25g

Fulfilling Liver Detox Salad with Ginger-Lemon Dressing

Time: 10 minutes
Servings: 2

Salad Ingredients:

- 2 cups of green cabbage, shredded
- 2 cups of purple cabbage, shredded
- 1 large carrot, shredded
- A large bunch of fresh parsley, roughly chopped
- 1/2 medium avocado, ripe and sliced
- 2 tablespoons of raisins or dried cranberries

Lemon-Ginger Salad Dressing Ingredients:

- inch fresh ginger, minced
- 1 medium garlic clove, crushed or finely minced
- 2 tablespoons of raw honey
- 1/2 cup of extra-virgin olive oil or coconut oil
- 3/4 cups of freshly squeezed lemon juice

Instructions:

1. In a bowl, add the minced ginger, minced garlic, honey, extra-virgin olive oil, and freshly squeezed lemon juice. Mix until well combined and set aside.
2. In another bowl, add all the salad ingredients and toss until well combined.
3. Drizzle with the lemon-ginger dressing and stir until well combined.
4. Serve and enjoy!

Nutritional information per serving:

- Calories: 673
- Total Fat: 61.1g
- Total Carbohydrate: 35.8g
- Dietary Fiber: 8.2g
- Protein: 4g

Spinach and Cranberry Salad with Almonds

Time: 10 minutes
Servings: 8

Salad Ingredients:

- 2 cups of fresh baby spinach
- 1 cup of toasted almonds, sliced
- 1 cup of dried cranberries

Sesame Seed Dressing Ingredients:

- 1 tablespoon of shallot, finely minced
- 2 tablespoons of toasted sesame seeds
- 1/4 cup of white wine vinegar
- 2 tablespoons of organic apple cider vinegar
- 1/2 cup of extra-virgin olive oil
- 3 tablespoons of pure raw honey
- 1 tablespoon of poppy seeds

Instructions:

1. In a bowl, add all the salad dressing ingredients and stir until well blended together.
2. In a large bowl, add the fresh baby spinach, toasted sliced almonds, and dried cranberries. Toss until well combined.
3. Drizzle with the salad dressing and stir until well combined.
4. Serve and enjoy!

Nutritional information per serving:

- Calories: 351
- Total Fat: 25g
- Total Carbohydrate: 29.1g
- Dietary Fiber: 3.98g
- Protein: 4.73g

Side Dishes and Desserts Recipes

Homemade Fruit Popsicles

Time: 3 hours
Servings: 6

Ingredients:

- 2 cups of fresh or frozen fruits
- 2 tablespoons of pure raw honey or other alternative sweeteners
- 2 tablespoons of freshly squeezed lemon juice
- 1/4 cup of low-fat milk, Greek yogurt, coconut cream or water juice

Instructions:

1. In a blender, add the frozen fruits, pure raw honey, lemon juice, and low-fat milk. Blend until smooth and silky.
2. Transfer the mixture to popsicle molds and place inside your freezer.
3. Allow to freeze for 2 to 3 hours.
4. Serve and enjoy!

Nutritional information per serving:

- Calories: 68
- Total Fat: 0.4g
- Total Carbohydrate: 11.1g
- Dietary Fiber: 0.8g
- Protein: 0.9g

Incredibly Fudgy Brownies

Time: 35 minutes
Servings: 16

Ingredients:

- 9 tablespoons of coconut oil or unsalted butter
- 1 tablespoon of coconut cream
- 2/3 to 1 cup of powdered erythritol or coconut sugar
- 3/4 cups of unsweetened cocoa powder
- 3/4 cups of almond flour
- 1/2 teaspoon of fine sea salt
- 2 large organic eggs

Instructions:

1. Preheat your oven to 350 degrees Fahrenheit.
2. Line a baking 8x8-inch baking pan with parchment paper and spray nonstick cooking spray.
3. In a medium bowl, add the coconut oil or butter, unsweetened cocoa powder, and fine sea salt. Mix well.
4. Whisk in the eggs, one at a time until

well combined.

5. Stir in the powdered erythritol and almond flour, whisk until well combined.
6. Pour the brownie batter to the baking pan and place inside your oven.
7. Bake for 16 to 26 minutes or until a toothpick comes out clean from the center.
8. Remove from your oven and allow to cool.
9. Serve and enjoy!

Nutritional information per serving:

- Calories: 104
- Total Fat: 10.3g
- Total Carbohydrates: 4g
- Dietary Fiber: 2.1g
- Protein: 2.4g

Chocolate Cake

Time: 50 minutes
Servings: 24

Ingredients:

- 1 cup of coconut flour
- 1 cup of unsweetened cocoa powder
- 1 1/2 cup of erythritol or coconut sugar or another sweetener
- 1 teaspoon of ground cinnamon powder
- 1/2 teaspoon of fine sea salt
- 2 teaspoons of baking powder
- 2 teaspoons of baking soda
- 1/2 cup of coconut oil
- 8 large pasture-raised eggs, beaten
- 4 cups of zucchini, finely grated
- 2 teaspoons of vanilla extract
- 3/4 cups of semisweet chocolate chips

Chocolate Cream Ingredients:

- 1 cup of softened butter
- 1 cup of powdered erythritol
- 2/3 cups of unsweetened cocoa powder
- 1/4 cups of unsweetened coconut milk
- 2 teaspoons of vanilla extract

Instructions:

1. Preheat your oven to 350 degrees Fahrenheit.
2. Line a baking pan with parchment paper and spray with nonstick cooking spray
3. In a large bowl, add the coconut flour, unsweetened cocoa powder, cinnamon, baking powder, baking soda, and fine sea salt.
4. Whisk in the coconut oil, vanilla extract, and eggs until well combined.
5. Stir in the finely grated zucchini
6. Transfer the cake to the baking pan and place inside your oven.
7. Bake for around 32 to 45 minutes or until a toothpick comes out clean

from the center.

8. Remove from your oven and allow to cool.
9. Spread the chocolate cream frosting over the cake.
10. To make the chocolate cream, add the softened butter, powdered erythritol, cocoa powder, coconut milk, and vanilla extract to a large bowl. Stir until well blended together.
11. Spread the chocolate cream over the cake.
12. Serve and enjoy!

Nutritional information per serving:

- Calories: 98
- Total Fat: 8.1g
- Carbohydrates: 6g
- Dietary Fiber: 3.4g
- Protein: 3.8g

Italian Cream Cake

Time: 1 hour and 30 minutes
Servings: 16

Ingredients:

- 1/2 cup of softened butter
- 1 cup of swerve sweetener or other sweetener alternatives
- 4 large pasture-raised eggs, egg yolks and egg whites separated
- 1/2 cup of organic heavy cream
- 1 teaspoon of vanilla extract
- 1 1/2 cup of almond flour or coconut flour
- 1/2 cup of unsweetened coconut flakes
- 1/2 cup of toasted pecans, chopped
- 1 teaspoon of baking powder
- 1 teaspoon of baking soda
- 1/2 teaspoon of fine sea salt

Frosting Ingredients:

- 1 (8-ounce) package of cream cheese, softened
- 1/2 cup of butter, softened
- 1 teaspoon of vanilla extract
- 1/2 cup of heavy whipping cream
- 1 cup of powdered swerve sweetener or other sweetener alternatives

Instructions:

1. Preheat your oven to 325 degrees Fahrenheit.
2. Line an 8-inch cake pan with parchment paper and spray with nonstick cooking spray
3. In a large bowl, add the 1/2 cup of softened butter and swerve sweetener. Beat until well combined.
4. Beat in the egg yolks and stir in the heavy cream and vanilla extract.
5. In the second bowl, add the egg yolks and the 1/4 teaspoon of the cream of tartar. Set aside.
6. In a third bowl, add the almond flour, unsweetened coconut flakes, toasted

chopped pecans, coconut flour, baking powder, baking soda, and fine sea salt. Add to the butter mixture and beat until well combined.

7. Gently fold in the egg white mixture to the cake batter.
8. Transfer the cake batter to the baking pan and place inside your oven.
9. Bake for 36 to 47 minutes or until the edges are golden.
10. Remove the cake pan from your oven and allow to cool.
11. To make the frosting: In a large bowl, add the softened cream cheese and butter. Beat until smooth.
12. Beat in the vanilla extract and swerve sweetener.
13. Gradually add in the heavy whipping cream and beat until well combined.
14. Spread the frosting cream over the cake.
15. Serve and enjoy!

Nutritional information per serving:

- Calories: 338
- Total Fat: 32g
- Total Carbohydrate: 6g
- Dietary Fiber: 2.9g
- Protein: 6.4g

Mint Chip Ice Cream

Time: 5 minutes + freezing time
Servings: 2

Ingredients:

- 2 medium frozen bananas, ripe and sliced
- 1/2 cup of coconut cream
- 1/4 cup of raw cashews
- 3 tablespoons of semisweet chocolate chips
- A dash of fine sea salt
- 1/8 teaspoon of pure peppermint extract

Instructions:

1. Add the frozen bananas slices, coconut cream, cashews, sea salt and peppermint extract to a blender.
2. Blend until smooth.
3. Gently fold in the semisweet chocolate chips
4. Transfer to a container and freeze for 4 hours or overnight until firm.
5. Serve and enjoy!

Nutritional information per serving:

- Calories: 426
- Total Fat: 27.3g
- Total Carbohydrate: 45.2g
- Dietary Fiber: 5.4g
- Protein: 7.2g

Strawberry Cheesecake

Time: 20 minutes + refrigerating time
Servings: 8

Ingredients:

- 1 pound of cream cheese, softened
- 1 cup of granulated Splenda or alternative sweeteners
- 2 large pasture-raised eggs
- 1 to 1/2 teaspoon of fresh lemon zest
- 1 to 1/2 teaspoon of fresh orange zest
- 1 tablespoon of heavy cream
- 1 teaspoon of pure vanilla extract
- Fresh strawberries
- Strawberry jam, melted

Instructions:

1. Preheat your oven to 350 degrees Fahrenheit. Grease a 6-inch cake pan with nonstick cooking spray
2. In a large bowl, add the cream cheese and granulated Splenda. Use an electric mixer and beat until smooth.
3. Beat in the eggs, lemon zest, orange zest, heavy cream, and pure vanilla extract.
4. Transfer the cheesecake batter into the cake pan and use a spatula to smooth the top.
5. Place inside your oven and bake for 10 minutes.
6. Reduce the heat to 275 degrees Fahrenheit and bake for an additional hour or until the edges are brown.

Remove from the oven.

7. Place the cheesecake inside your refrigerator and allow to cool.
8. Top the cheesecake with the strawberry jam and fresh strawberries.
9. Serve and enjoy!

Nutritional information per serving:

- Calories: 225
- Total Fat: 24g
- Total Carbohydrate: 11g
- Dietary Fiber: 1.1g
- Protein: 7g

Blueberry Almond Crisp

Time: 1 hour
Servings: 6

Ingredients:

- 6 cups of fresh or frozen blueberries, rinsed with water
- 3 tablespoons of cornstarch
- 2 tablespoons of pure maple syrup
- 1 tablespoon of unsalted butter, melted
- 1 teaspoon of organic ground cinnamon
- 1/4 cup of almond flour
- 3/4 cups of old-fashioned oats
- 2 teaspoons of almond extract
- 1 teaspoon of coconut oil or nonstick cooking spray

Instructions:

1. Preheat your oven to 350 degrees Fahrenheit.
2. Grease an 8-inch square baking pan with 1 teaspoon of coconut oil or nonstick cooking spray.
3. In a bowl, add the old-fashioned oats, almond flour, and organic ground cinnamon. Stir until well combined.
4. Add the 2 tablespoons of pure maple syrup and 1 tablespoon of unsalted butter continue to stir until well combined. Set aside.
5. In another bowl, add the 6 cups of fresh or frozen blueberries, 3 tablespoons of cornstarch and 2 teaspoons of almond extract. Stir until well combined.
6. Transfer the blueberry mixture to the square baking pan and sprinkle with the oat topping.
7. Place inside your oven and bake for 55 to 65 minutes.
8. Remove from your oven and allow to cool. Serve and enjoy!

Nutritional information per serving:

- Calories: 125
- Total Fat: 4.2g
- Total Carbohydrate: 24g
- Dietary Fiber: 4.3g
- Protein: 1.8g

Drinks Recipes

Iced Dandelion Lime Tea

Time: 3 hours and 15 minutes
Servings: 8

Ingredients:

- 1 quart of freshly picked dandelion flowers, yellow parts separated and rinsed
- 1 cup of hot water
- 3 quarts of cold iced water
- 1/2 cup organic dried red raspberry leaves
- 3 tablespoons of dried stevia leaf or alternative sweeteners
- 1/2 cup of dried red raspberry leaves
- 4 medium limes, juiced

Instructions:

1. In a bowl, add the dried stevia leaf and dried red raspberry leaf. Pour in the 1 cup of hot water and allow to steep for 5 to 8 minutes.
2. Transfer the liquid to a glass jar.
3. Stir in the lime juice and ice cold water.
4. Mix in the dandelion flowers and refrigerate for 3 to 4 hours.
5. Serve and enjoy!

Nutritional information per serving:

- Calories: 5
- Total Fat: 0g
- Total Carbohydrate: 1.5g
- Dietary Fiber: 0.5g
- Protein: 0.1g

Turmeric Lemon-Ginger Tea

Time: 15 minutes
Servings: 1

Ingredients:

- 1-1/2 cup of water
- 1 teaspoon of turmeric root, freshly grated OR 1/2 teaspoon of organic turmeric powder
- 1 teaspoon of ginger root, freshly grated OR 1/2 teaspoon of ginger powder
- 1/2 medium-sized lemon, juiced and zest
- 1 tablespoon of raw honey
- 2 twists of fresh black pepper
- A fine dash of sea salt

Instructions:

1. In a saucepan over medium-high heat, add the grated turmeric, lemon zest, grated ginger, and water.
2. Bring to a simmer and allow to heat through for 5 to 10 minutes. Be careful not to bring to a boil.
3. Strain the liquid using a fine mesh strainer and transfer the liquid to a serving glass.
4. Stir in the lemon juice and honey.
5. Serve and enjoy!

Nutritional information per serving:

- Calories: 86
- Total Fat: 0.4g
- Total Carbohydrate: 22.6g
- Dietary Fiber: 1.5g
- Protein: 0.7g

Effective Liver Detox Smoothie

Time: 10 minutes
Servings: 1

Ingredients:

- 1 medium banana, ripe and peeled
- 1/2 medium green apple, cored and roughly chopped
- 1 medium-sized carrot, peeled and roughly chopped
- 1 large handful of fresh baby spinach
- 1 teaspoon of turmeric root, peeled and minced OR 1/2 teaspoon of organic turmeric powder
- 1 tablespoon of fresh parsley, finely chopped
- 1/2 medium-sized lemon, juiced
- A small pinch of organic ground cinnamon powder
- 3/4 cups of unsweetened almond milk or unsweetened coconut milk

Instructions:

1. In a blender, add all the ingredients and blend until smooth.
2. Transfer the contents to a serving glass.
3. Serve and enjoy!

Nutritional information per serving:

- Calories: 348
- Total Fat: 22.7g
- Total Carbohydrate: 36.4g
- Dietary Fiber: 10g
- Protein: 8.2g

Essential Liver and Kidney Cleansing Green Juice

Time: 5 minutes
Servings: 2

Ingredients:

- 1-1/2 cup of water
- 1 large English cucumber, chopped
- 2 medium-sized lemons, skin removed
- 2 green apples, core removed
- 2 peaches, seed removed
- 3 cups of kale
- 1 cup of lettuce, chopped
- 1-inch fresh ginger, peeled

Instructions:

4. Add all the ingredients to a blender and blend until smooth.
5. Transfer the mixture into serving glasses and enjoy!

Nutritional information per serving:

- Calories: 329
- Total Fat: 1.4g
- Total Carbohydrate: 83.4g
- Dietary Fiber: 14.6g
- Protein: 7.2g

The Best Liver-Detox Apple Carrot Beet Ginger Juice

Time: 10 minutes
Servings: 2

Ingredients:

- 1 medium green apple, skin and core removed
- 4 medium carrots, peeled and cleaned
- 1 medium red beetroot, peeled and diced
- 1 (1-inch) piece of fresh ginger root, peeled and finely grated
- 2 large handfuls of fresh baby spinach or kale
- 1 English cucumber, washed and peeled
- 1/2 lemon, peeled and seeded
- 1/2 lime, peeled and seeded
- A dash of fine sea salt

Instructions:

6. In a blender, add all the ingredients and blend until smooth.
7. Place a fine mesh strainer over a bowl and add the blended mixture.
8. Press down the ingredients until most of the liquid goes through. Alternatively, you can consume the juicing contents.
9. Transfer the juiced liquid to serving glasses.
10. Serve and enjoy!

Nutritional information per serving:

- Calories: 234
- Total Fat: 1.8g
- Total Carbohydrate: 50.8g
- Dietary Fiber: 15g
- Protein: 12.9g

Conclusion

Thank you again for finishing the book, "The Liver Rescue Diet: The Solution to Psoriasis, Fatty Liver, Weight Issues, Acne, Diabetes, Strep, Gout, Gallstones Adrenal Stress, Eczema, Fatigue, SIBO, and Autoimmune Disease."

In this book, we have explored a wide variety of methods for improving the conditions of your liver. We have provided you with valuable information about your liver, liver-related disease and your best way to go up against it. You can live a healthy life and completely cure your liver-related disease before it advances into a more severe problem. We educate you on the best foods you should introduce your body and foods to avoid that will ultimately damage your liver. Take charge of your health now and reap the benefits of better health!

You can make the proper adjustments a little at a time to ease into a new lifestyle, or you can do an entire liver makeover! Whatever road you take, listen to your body and how it responds to these new changes. If you notice any problems that are too much for you, call your primary care doctor or schedule an appointment. Using the information here to construct a plan will amaze you by the results. And finally, this book comes with 70 incredibly delicious recipes which will satisfy your stomach and help your liver. With all of this at your leisure, it's almost impossible to fail.

On a final thought, if you enjoyed this book or find it valuable, I will like to ask you for a small favor. Can you consider taking the time to leave an honest review on Amazon? I wish to help as many people suffering from liver-related disease and your review will surely help me achieve this goal. Maybe you can recommend this guide to some of your friends and family. This will all be greatly appreciated.
Thank you and best of luck on your journey to better health and a better liver!

Appendix: Measurement Conversion Table for Cooking

Following recipes don't need to be complicated, especially if you are asked to double or halve the ingredients. The convenient measurement conversion chart below will help you accurately convert measurements while you are whipping up something in the kitchen. Everything from a dash of salt to a cup of water is presented to help you prepare the best dishes. Refer to this appendix measurement conversion chart whenever needed.

VOLUME CONVERSIONS

- 3 teaspoons = 1 tablespoons = 1/2 ounces = 1/16 cups = 15 milliliters = 0.015 liters
- 12 teaspoons = 4 tablespoons = 2 ounces = 1/4 cups = 60 milliliters = 0.06 liters
- 24 teaspoons = 8 tablespoons = 4 ounces = 1/2 cups = 125 milliliters = 0.125 liters
- 48 teaspoons = 16 tablespoons = 8 ounces = 1 cups = 1/2 pints = 1/4 quarts = 1/16 gallons = 250 milliliters = 0.25 liters
- 16 ounces = 2 cups = 1 pint = 1/2 quarts = 1/8 gallons = 500 milliliters = 0.5 liters
- 32 ounces = 4 cups = 2 pints = 1 quarts = 1/4 gallons = 950 milliliters = 0.95 liters
- 128 ounces = 16 cups = 8 pints = 4 quarts = 1 gallon = 3800 milliliters = 3.8 liters

QUICK CHEAT SHEET / VOLUME CONVERSIONS

- 1 tablespoon = 15 milliliters = 3 teaspoons
- 4 tablespoons = 60 milliliters = 1/4 cup
- 1 ounce = 30 milliliters = 2 tablespoons
- 1 cup = 250 milliliters = 8 ounces
- 1 pint = 500 milliliters = 2 cups
- 1 quart = 950 milliliters = 4 cups
- 1 quart = 950 milliliters = 2 pints
- 1 gallon = 3800 milliliters = 3.8 liters = 4 quarts

Appendix II: Useful Websites to Help You with the Liver Rescue Diet

The Internet is a vast place with tons of useful information that can help you improve liver function. Feel free to explore some of the useful websites below that will enhance your journey for a better liver.

https://liverfoundation.org/: The American Liver Foundation is an organization that educates and supports the people affected by liver disease and help fund research that can cure liver disease. The website also contains tons of useful information and inspirational stories.

https://www.webmd.com/: This health website provides information for anyone who is looking for reliable and quick information regarding weight loss, health conditions and diets. WebMD is one of the top-notched websites with well-researched reports and support made by weight loss experts.

https://consumerhealthdigest.com/: This website provides effective strategies and treatments to help fight with weight loss and health conditions.

https://health.yahoo.net/: The website contains well-researched and helpful information that can help you lose weight. It also contains a host of reports based on weight loss, diets and workout regimens. In addition, it also provides information regarding common diseases and ways to treat them.

Appendix III: Recommended Products for the Liver Rescue Diet

Are you looking for the best products to help fight liver disease? You can improve your liver function naturally with products designed to give beneficial results. Below you will find a list of the best products to help you repair your liver whether it's for cooking, supplements, workout equipment, or other specialty items. These products have helped others in the past and I hope it will for you too.

Must-Have Kitchen Appliances and Cookware

Here is a list of some of the best kitchen utensils and prep items that will surely save you time in the kitchen and enhance your overall cooking experience:

Crock Pot 6 Quart Programmable Cook and Carry Slow Cooker with Digital Timer

Mueller Ultra-Stick 500-Watt 9-Speed Powerful Immersion Multi-Purpose Blender

Brieftons Spiralizer

Cuisinart WAF-F20 Stainless Steel Waffle Maker

Instant Pot Ultra 6 Quart 10-in-1 Multi-Use Programmable Pressure Cooker

Breville BFP800XL Sous Chef Food Processor

Breville BCI600XL Smart Scoop Ice Cream Maker

Vitamix 5200 Blender Professional-Grade, 64-Ounce Container

Ninja Intelli-Sense Kitchen System (a cheaper alternative to the Vitamix)

Keurig K55 Coffee Maker

Sunbeam FPSBDLM920 Donut Maker

Cookware:

Stainless Steel Cookware Set, Pots and Pan Set

Pyrex Storage Container Set

Nylon Stainless Steel Kitchen Utensils Set

Lodge 10.25-inch Cast Iron Skillet

Lodge 6-Quart Iron Dutch Oven

Bellemain Porcelain Ramekins

Supplement Recommendations:

As we covered earlier in this book, taking supplements can help repair liver function. Below you will find a list of herbs and nutrients that can improve your overall liver performance, but also support your liver's detoxification mechanisms.

Amla Fruit Extract – Vibrant Health Super Natural C

L-Glutathione – NOW Foods Liver Refresh

Milk Thistle Extract – Enzymedica Purify Liver Detox

Burdock Root – Gaia Herbs Liver Cleanse

Chlorella – NovaForme CytoGreens for Athletes, Chocolate

CPSIA information can be obtained
at www.ICGtesting.com
Printed in the USA
LVHW102348110121
676217LV00013B/769

9 781637 839027